ADVENTURES IN PRAYER

C. Manly Morton

ADVENTURES IN PRAYER

FLEMING H. REVELL COMPANY
WESTWOOD, NEW JERSEY

Scripture passages quoted in this book are from *The Revised Standard Version of the Bible* (RSV), with some exceptions.

The Scripture passages quoted in Chapter 3 are from *The King James Version of the Bible* (KJV).

The American Standard Version of the Bible (ASV) is quoted several times.

Acknowledgment is given to McGraw-Hill Book Company for permission to use the lines from *A Man Called Peter* by Catherine Marshall.

COPYRIGHT © 1966 BY FLEMING H. REVELL COMPANY ● ALL RIGHTS RESERVED ● WESTWOOD, NEW JERSEY ● LIBRARY OF CONGRESS CATALOG CARD NUMBER: 66-12438 ● PRINTED IN THE UNITED STATES OF AMERICA ● 1.1

*To the tens of thousands of wonderful
Christian friends on two continents
who have shared a rich and inspiring
Prayer Fellowship with us, this little
volume is lovingly dedicated*

Preface

Writing this book has been a thrilling experience. I trust that the reader, will find in it something of interest and of lingering worth—something which will help and strengthen your prayer life, something which will make God, and communion with Him, more real and meaningful to you.

Prayer is so very personal. We can learn *about* prayer by reading books and by listening to the experiences of others; but we can only *learn to pray* through personal experience. The merits of prayer—its depth, its satisfactions and inspirations, its magnitude and power—can be realized only as we learn, through practice, to talk with our Heavenly Father and feel the greatness of His Being overshadow and possess us.

There have been five important and progressive steps in the development of my own prayer life. Each was brought about through facing a definite crisis and letting God lead me through it.

The first came when Mrs. Morton and I were left stranded in a strange country. It was in 1918. We had gone as the first missionaries of any organized Protestant group to the Republic of Paraguay, South America. We went without chart or compass. We were to spend the first year studying the situation; and then recommend a program of work. We did not know a soul in the country, and the whole atmosphere was suspicious and hostile to evangelical missions.

We arrived in Asunción on November 11, 1918, the day the

armistice was signed, ending World War I. We carried enough money to last us about thirty days. We were to receive a check each month, so we felt secure. But with the signing of the armistice, all of the ships between the United States and South America were diverted to Europe to transport our soldiers home. There was no airmail service in those days. The result was that we received no mail, and thus no checks, for two and a half months. Our mission board in the United States mailed the checks each month, but they kept piling up in New York. We kept writing, frantically asking what was wrong, but our letters were piling up in Buenos Aires. Neither our board nor we knew what was happening.

By the middle of December, our money was all gone. How we lived during the next six weeks, only God knows—we do not. The important thing, however, is that we did live, and came out of the experience physically well and greatly strengthened spiritually.

During the early days of this period we were frantic. We prayed more during those days than we had ever prayed before. At first God seemed a long way off; then He came nearer, and a reassuring calmness and peace came over us. Gradually we learned to pray: "God, we are in your hands. Lead us in the way we should go. Do not let us make any mistakes. Give us the strength, courage, and wisdom to meet each day as it arrives, and to close it in a way that will not bring injury or reproach on the cause we are here to represent."

We spent some days without food, but for some reason we were never discouraged or downhearted. In a way we had never experienced before, God was close to us. We felt an inner presence of the Holy Spirit which both astonished us and brought complete confidence to us.

While there were days of hunger and deadlines beyond which we could neither see nor imagine a single ray of light, there was never a moment when we were embarrassed, or when our mission was placed in jeopardy. Our closest friends did not realize what our situation was during those days and weeks. "Coincidences," the cynic might call our achievements, but for the believer in God there is but one explanation—they were miracles. As we look back upon them now, they seem so simple and natural; but we know that they were the doings of God.

Through this rugged experience, we learned the first great lesson in prayer—*Prayer is the putting of self in God's hands and trusting Him to do what is best. Have faith in God, and do not worry.*

The second crisis occurred at the end of our first furlough, when we were asked to go to Puerto Rico instead of returning to Paraguay. Not only had we invested some of the most vital years of our lives among the Paraguayan people, but we had also learned to love and appreciate them. We had sown the first seeds; we had formulated both the short- and the long-range plans for the development of the work needed there. We had established International College (Colegio Internacional), and had gone through both the agonies and the joys of "making brick without straw" in the founding of that school. We had lived close to the boys and girls, being both father and mother to them. Thinking that I was to spend the rest of my life in that country, I had entered the University of Paraguay Law School in order to improve my knowledge about the language and customs of the country and to establish better relationships with the future leaders of the country. We felt that we were especially prepared for the tasks ahead, and we wanted to continue.

Then the message came: "We need you in Puerto Rico." The Union Evangelical Seminary was just three years old.

The Disciples of Christ, the church with which I was affiliated, had never had a representative on the faculty; they needed one—someone who already knew the Spanish language. I had had experience in teaching, so the lot fell to me. Of course, I could have said "no," and if I had been contrary enough, perhaps the Board would have given in and said, "All right, go back to Paraguay."

But I wonder if I would ever have been happy under those conditions. I could only feel that perhaps God was leading those who had made the decision and perhaps I needed to let Him lead me, but the "self" within me was reluctant to make the change.

The day and night after receiving the notice of transfer, I spent on a train going from Indianapolis to Estes Park, Colorado. I have never spent a more miserable 24 hours. I neither ate nor slept. I tried to pray, but found that it was difficult to make contact with God. I felt so alone and so helpless; I was tempted to throw the whole thing aside, accept the call to a very good church which had come to me a few days before, and go my own way.

Just before we reached Denver, my mind and body began to relax. For a few minutes (it seemed like hours) I was in the "twilight zone" between wakefulness and sleep. Then the wall between God and me started to crumble away, and I heard the silent voice of God saying: "Are you ready to let Me come in and take over now?" And my mind and heart responded: "Yes, Lord. Not my will, but Thine, be done."

I was still not sure that God wanted me to go to Puerto Rico, but I was sure that I was going to seek and follow His guidance. From that moment on, prayer became more real to me, and decisions were made more easily. Since that time, I have not tried to carry the whole burden in any endeavor; I have labored to do my part, but I have also fought to keep my selfish will in subjection and at all times to say: "God, You know best. This is what I want to do, but You know a lot more than I do. If I am wrong in what I want to do, You set me right. If what I am asking is not for the best, please do not give it to me. Not my will, but Thine, be done."

I have never doubted that going to Puerto Rico was the right thing to do, and I have never doubted that it was God who directed the decision. Through this experience, I learned the lesson—*In times of decision, let God take over.*

The third spiritual crisis came several years later. The depression of the early thirties was especially severe in Puerto Rico. Even the "normal" economic level of the people of the island was exceedingly low—normally, more than half of them went to bed hungry every night. The average per capita annual income was less than $150. Most of our evangelical Christians were from the lower-income ranks, and our ministers were all on a subsistence basis. Through our mission board we received $1,240 per month for the support of our entire mission. This was to cover travel, scholarships, literature, maintenance of buildings—and support for our eighteen ministers and their families.

Early in 1933 we received word that our subsidy would have to be cut by 65 percent—from $1240 to $440 a month. This while our needs were increasing! What the churches in the U.S. had been contributing for ministerial support had been drastically reduced, and our Puerto Rican Christians were plunged deeper into the abyss of need and hunger. There was a real temptation to blame God—to cry out: "Lord, why are You forsaking Your people?"

The double load of feeling hungry and watching others go hungry brought us almost to the breaking point. Many of our members and ministers did break. A wave of emotionalism swept over our churches; there were excessess of trances, speaking in tongues, holy dances, prophecies, all-night meetings. Illiterate men and women—some sincere, some social and spiritual tramps—moved freely among our people, confusing their minds and spirits. We were afraid the work of thirty-five years might be lost.

We worked as never before. We thought we knew exactly what was needed—this wave of emotionalism had to be rooted-out completely. We prayed earnestly; but again, the connection with God seemed to be broken. We made several blunders and caused a number of heartaches.

At last God came through to us, and said: "Before you can truly pray to Me, before I can help you, you must learn to have patience with your brother. You must try harder to understand your fellow Christian and the trying experiences he is facing. Go out and live closer to these, My children. Be patient with them and love them. They are mistaken in some things, but so are you in other things. Humble yourself and learn to understand."

We did that. Slowly, things began to take proper shape. The churches which survived that trying time are different from the cold, unresponsive churches we have found elsewhere. They are filled with a fervent, evangelistic spirit, which, within two decades, has moved the Disciples of Christ from sixth to second place among the most active evangelistic church groups in Puerto Rico.

God taught us that to pray effectively, *we must be patient and understanding with our brethren; we must live close to them and love them.* ". . . he that loveth not his brother whom he hath seen, how can he love God whom he hath not seen?" (I JOHN 4:20, KJV). Love is not a matter of words; love casts out suspicion and misunderstanding, breaks down barriers, and makes all things possible. God taught us that to pray effectively we must be able to say truly "our Father," not just "my Father."

The fourth crisis came out of our efforts to solve the problem mentioned above. In order to work ourselves out of the confusion and error into which our people had fallen, we realized the necessity of having a place where we could gather our ministers, laymen, and young people in small groups and teach them patiently, lovingly, ". . . precept upon precept, precept upon precept, line upon line, line upon line, here a little, there a little . . ." (ISAIAH 28:10), until we could come to a clearer understanding—we realized that we must have a place set apart from the confusion of the mass of people, where we could talk to God and let God speak to us.

To meet these needs, McLean Conference Grounds was established. For its beginning, we had four acres of ground, an old, dilapidated, five-room cottage, and four-hundred and fifteen dollars. But God was with us. The first year we were able to build two cottages. Attendance grew. The effect on the life of our churches was gradual, but pronounced. A summer school for ministers was started. The first year 18 attended; the next year 45 applied for admission, but there was room for less than half that number. Young people were responding to our call in far greater numbers than we had ever anticipated. At last it seemed that we were "on top of the world." God was blessing us abundantly.

But then the "fountains" of God's blessings seemed to dry up. The people were responding, but our capacity to take care of them was not expanding. We needed more cottages, more beds, chairs, tables, etc. Up to that point, God had showered blessings upon us—not only had money come from unexpected sources (from people and places we had never heard of before), but the Conference Grounds was accomplishing more than we had even hoped; gradually, and creatively, the problems which were disrupting our churches were being solved; a great hope had taken hold of us. Suddenly, there was a reversal of all this—a complete paralysis of development had set in. For some reason, our prayers were not getting through to God. We prayed just as earnestly and with as much faith, but nothing but silence came back from God. By that time in my life, I thought I had had a great deal of experience in prayer. I had seen some marvelous things take place. Now I was discouraged, beaten, and I cried out to God: "O God, what have I done? In what way have I offended You? Please open the door and set me right."

That night, discouraged and feeble of faith, I sat down at my typewriter with the intention of writing to twenty of the ministers who wanted to come to summer school and telling them that there was no room for them.

At last God started answering that last anguished appeal. He started telling me what was really wrong with me; it hit me pretty hard at first, but I had asked for it, and was determined to accept it.

I called Mrs. Morton into the office and said: "Sit down. There is something I must talk with you about." There must have been something peculiar about my expression or my manner, because a puzzled look came over her face. I said: "For months we have been praying for funds with which to erect two more cottages, so that we can accept all who want to attend summer school and so that we can expand our youth conferences, but God has been deaf to our pleadings. I think I have discovered the reason why." The puzzled look on her face became more pronounced, and she responded with a questioning "Yes?" "Well," I continued, "I have a paid-up insurance policy, which I took out when I was a bachelor preacher twenty-five years ago. It is now worth several thousands of dollars. All I have to do is write a letter and return the signed policy, and then we will have that much money for the cottages we need."

"But," she said, "you are not thinking of using that! We have been saving that for a little home when retirement comes. That is all we have—it is prehaps all we will ever have."

"Yes, I know," I answered, "but I think that is why God is not blessing us right now. For months we have been telling God that the most important thing we can think of is the development of this Conference Grounds, and we have been asking Him to open the way for our needs to be filled; but deep down in our hearts we have been telling ourselves that holding on to that money is more important. God has been reading our hearts, instead of being fooled by our words; our lives and our words are not in harmony. They have to be, before we can really pray."

Tears came to her eyes. At the time, I thought they were tears of regret, but now I know they were tears of joy—tears which come when one gets really close to God.

The result was that I cashed the policy, ordered lumber, called workmen, and started the erection of new cottages. That money was every penny we had; it was all we ever hoped to have. But from that day forward, McLean Conference Grounds has never lacked for a thing, and God has opened the "windows" of heaven and blessed Mrs. Morton and me, both spiritually and materially, in ways we had never dreamed.

This crisis, or adventure in prayer, taught us that *our lives and our prayers have to be in harmony*. What we say in prayer has very little importance—it is what is uppermost in our hearts that really matters to God. God does not do for us that which we can do for ourselves; but He never fails to take over when we have exhausted our own resources—when He is really needed.

The fifth, and perhaps the greatest, crisis in my prayer life came at the time of retirement. There is no more critical period in a person's life than this. For one who has lived an active life and gets deep-seated happiness out of his work, the thought of retirement is disconcerting—frustrating. Under the strain of it, some people die within a few short years and others break mentally, while others just wither and impatiently wait for the end, or grow cynical and become a burden to themselves and everyone about them.

At sixty-seven (mandatory retirement age for missionaries), I was as well as and could do as strenuous a day's work as when I was fifty. It was difficult to understand why I could not go on with the work to which I had dedicated my life, in which I had invested so many of my years.

I, like most other people, was a bit resentful and somewhat lost. I considered going into some other line of work. My nephew had a bakery, and I asked him for a job behind the counter. He was wiser than I thought, because he just seemed not to hear me. He knew that I would not be happy doing that kind of work. He knew that I had something which God still needed.

I am sure that some of my disappointments and resentments crept into my prayers, because there was another period during which it was impossible to reach God satisfyingly. My soul was greatly troubled. Then God gradually began to teach me a new lesson. Gradually He challenged me to a form of service which has brought me indescribable joy and satisfaction, and which has given me the feeling that perhaps my most vital, fruitful years have been those since retirement.

During this period, God has used me in the establishing of one new church, which in the short period of seven years has become one of the most rapidly growing and effective churches in the state of Florida. He has used me in helping to put three other churches on their feet, and in serving ad interim ministeries in ten other churches. He has used me in having very close relationships with young people, and in helping to guide and strengthen more than a score into full-time Christian service. He has guided me in my most effective preaching, and in a most satisfying struggle to work out an understanding of spiritual truths.

God has taught me this—*Don't look backward or clutter up your life with regrets and resentments. Do not waste your energies fighting against that which cannot be changed. Live for today, and you will find plenty to do—and not only that, you will find life exciting, satisfying, and rewarding. Put into your work all that you have of interest, enthusiasm, hope, faith, determination, and love. Then when the night comes, thank God and go to sleep.*

It is on the background of the above experiences that these chapters have been written. Humbly, I ask your forgiveness for putting so much of myself in it. I desired otherwise, but how can one write, especially on such an intimate subject, without being guided and controlled by his own experiences.

This book has been written with a prayer in my heart. Please read it with a prayer in yours. And no matter how much or how little you understand about prayer, keep in mind that you still need to pray: "Lord, teach us to pray."

Contents

	Preface	7
1	Why Should I Pray?	23
2	What Is Prayer?	33
3	Lord, Teach Us to Pray	40
4	Whatsoever You Ask in His Name	60
5	Prayer for the Sick	67
6	Should We Pray for Faith?	80
7	Prayer and Self-Surrender	92
8	Through Prayer, Victory	100
9	Summary	110

ADVENTURES IN PRAYER

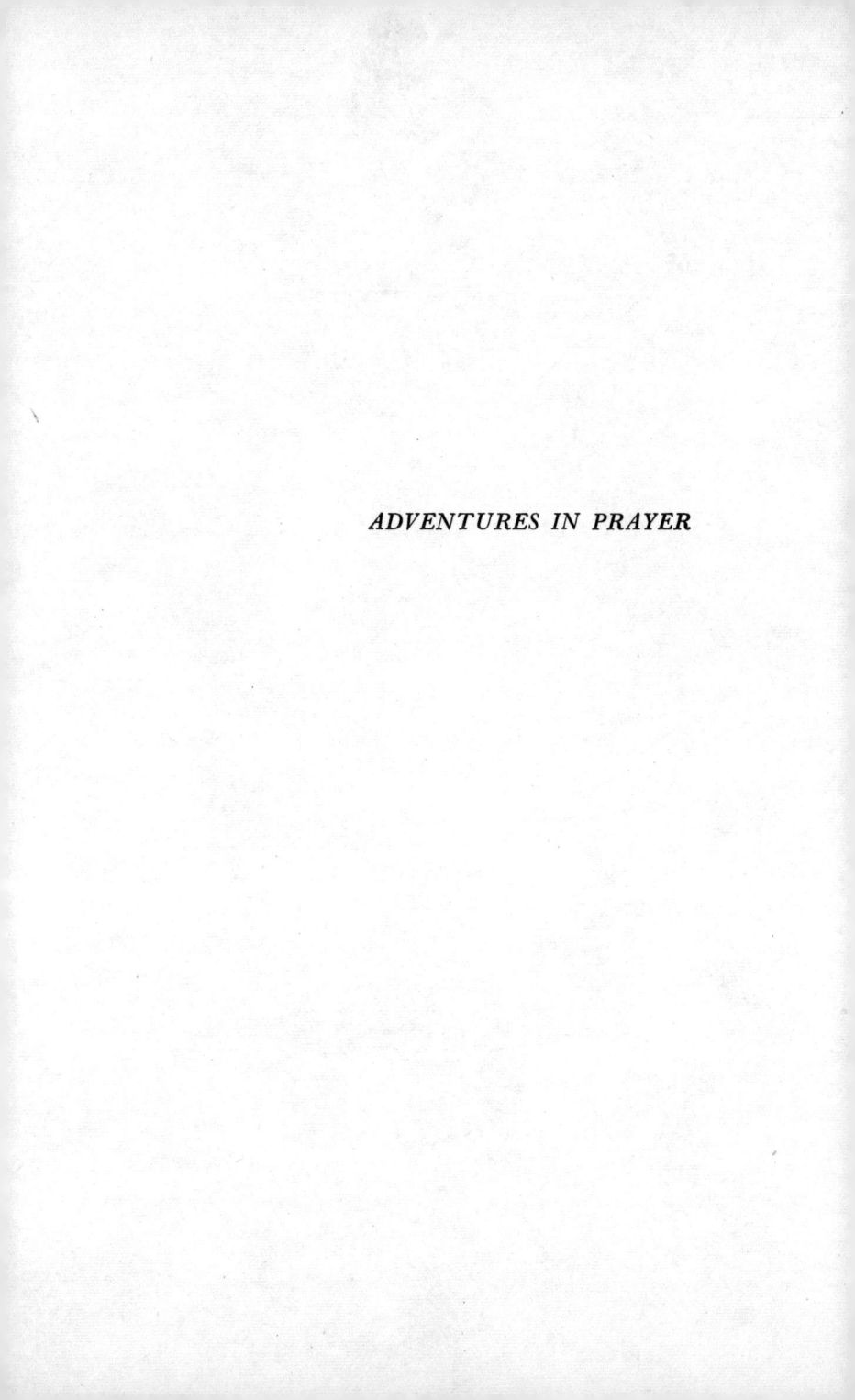

1. WHY SHOULD I PRAY?

SUSAN SNOWDEN OPENED the door as though she resented it being there. Usually bright and cheerful, there was a deep seriousness about her manner that day. Without saying "Good morning," and even before she could be seated, she burst out with the questions: "Dr. Morton, why should I pray? What is the good of it? What should I expect from it?"

Naturally, I was stunned. Susan Snowden was one of the finest Christian girls I had ever known. She was clean in her living, wholesome in her thinking, and was a tireless worker in church activities. On the campus of the university, where she was a senior, she was a recognized leader in all religious activities, as well as an outstanding student. In her church she was a sponsor of the youth-fellowship group, taught in the Bible school, and sang in the choir. I could not imagine her with a problem of this kind, and for a moment it stunned me.

Her next question brought me back to my senses: "What is prayer, anyway? And how should one pray?"

I noted a tear in her eyes; and a tremor was creeping into her voice. Automatically, I reached over and touched her hand, and found myself saying, "Susan, let us pray for a moment."

It was a rather crude, bungling prayer, for in that moment I found that I myself did not know how to pray. But there was one thing I was very sure of—that there is power in prayer; whenever we are facing a "chasm" which we alone cannot cross, prayer can build a bridge.

At the end of the prayer I said: "Susan, tell me about it. What has disturbed you? Let's talk it over for a bit."

"It was at that workshop," the girl went on to say. "Up to then I held to what you might call a rather 'naive' faith in prayer. I had never tried to analyze it or formulate definitions. But at the workshop something happened to me. The more the leaders tried to explain 'prayer,' the more confused I became." She paused and wiped a tear from her eye.

"Then, when I went home and started a 'prayer cell' among the girls of my dormitory, I started asking myself questions as to what I was endeavoring to accomplish. I found the girls praying for new dresses when they had a closet full already. I found them praying that they might get a date with a certain boy on campus. I found them praying that they might pass their exams, and get good grades. I found them looking on god as a kind of Santa Claus, and my faith in prayer took a nose dive."

"I want you to help me, Dr. Morton. And, more than that, I want you to come over and talk to my prayer group. I have been miserable since I have been trying to lead others down a 'pathway' which I realize I never really knew myself."

I knew that Susan Snowden was not alone in her questionings about prayer. Hundreds of others had been to visit me—especially young people—with the same misgivings, the same fears, the same desperate desire for something which they felt was slipping away from them.

My own life has not been free from the same struggle. And even after more than half a century of trying to lead men and women to Christ, I feel that there is much I still do not understand. Indeed, all of us "see through a glass darkly," and there is no reproach for admitting ignorance of the depth and fullness of the great mysteries of God.

It is "sin" only when one stops adventuring—either because he feels that he has learned all of the answers, or because of a feeling of frustration and defeat. It is "sin" only when one stops following the "gleam"—when he ceases to be fascinated by the mysteries of God's greatness, and loses his hunger and thirst for an increasing understanding of the eternal truths of God.

Many people are discouraged because they cannot understand all of the intricate mysteries of God and his universe after ten easy lessons. Too many times they say: "I cannot understand God." Therefore, they stop trying, and become indifferent to his existence. They fail to realize that in order to understand God, they would have to be as great as, or greater than, He—then God would not be God at all.

They fail to understand life and its great spiritual implications and possibilities. And because they cannot easily understand it all, they cease to think—they kill within them the spirit of adventure which God gave them to inspire and drive them on.

Prayer is the greatest resource of the human soul—and yet man understands so little about it. The trouble is not with prayer, but with man and his limited understanding and experience.

I found in Susan Snowden a spirit who was willing to adventure. When she saw that I, too, had problems, that I had not the answers to all of her questions, and that after fifty years of study and earnest experimenting with great religious truths I was still a pilgrim, she was enthusiastically willing to go adventuring with me.

The present chapters were prepared originally for Susan Snowden, in the effort to answer her questions. They were then used with her prayer group, and since then have been used with other individuals and groups. Their success in these cases and the requests of many friends have convinced me that they may be of service to a much larger group. The questions treated herein are questions asked by Susan and her group of friends.

We trust that you, the reader, if you have had questionings—and who has not—will find something which will be of value to you. If you do, do not fail to bow your head, and say "Thank you, God."

Together, let us go adventuring. The first question we will examine is: "Why should I pray?" Perhaps this is the most basic of all questions concerning prayer.

Man prays because he cannot help it—by nature, he is a praying being. No matter what his intellectual status or his social station in life, no matter what his religion, or whether he admits to a religious faith or not, there are moments in the life of every mature human being when he cries out, for either relief or fulfillment, to a "force" outside of, and greater than, himself.

But this answer is too rudimentary—too distantly related to what we usually mean when we speak of "prayer."

Many people pray through habit—it is what Christians are supposed to do. Like the Tibetan who spins his prayer wheel, or the Japanese who flies his prayer flag, many people seem to feel that there is a magic in prayer—the act of going through a certain ritual. They would feel spiritually "undressed" without it.

Parents are mainly responsible for this attitude. Most parents teach their children to "say" a prayer; very few teach their children to "pray." And there is a world of difference between "saying" and "praying."

But not only are children taught to "say" their prayers, they also are taught to "say" them to father or mother. How often do we hear a tired, distraught, busy mother say to her husband: "Dear, will you hear Johnny's prayers?"

The prayer is something Johnny has learned, and he "repeats" it to father or mother. Without father or mother there to "hear" his prayer, he is lost, and is apt to skip it entirely and slip into bed with a slightly guilty conscience.

Doubtless, a little, memorized prayer is very useful for the very young child, but it should be more a point of departure—a starting point—for a fuller and constantly growing awareness of God and fellowship with Him through personal prayer.

A child of four or five years of age can understand much more than we give him credit for. With his vivid imagination, he is much more capable than we think of understanding spiritual things.

Instead of taking thirty seconds to "hear" him "say" his prayers, then giving him a peck on the cheek and a pat on the bottom, and telling him to go to sleep, it would be "worlds" better to take five or ten minutes away from the other things of life, no matter how important we think they are, and talk with him (on his experience level, of course) about God and what it really means to "pray." When that is done, the two—parent and child—should pray a few words together.

For some reason, most Christian leaders seem to take it for granted that people automatically will understand prayer—its nature, its purpose, the fullness of its beauty, fruitfulness, and blessings. Even the public prayers in our church services are so often perfunctory—taken for granted, as a necessary, although not a very enjoyable or fruitful, part of every formal service, without interest to the ordinary layman in the pew.

Perhaps this is the principal reason why so many people who grew up in Christian homes and as children were taught to "say" their prayers regularly, neglect in later life even to think of praying except when there comes a crisis in their lives or they need some material thing.

A short time ago I had a pathetic letter from a fine Christian woman who had just lost her husband. They both had been active church members all of their lives—she had played the organ, and he had served as an elder for forty years. Now, she was deeply troubled—she wondered if her husband was "saved," she wondered if she was "saved," and she was going through torment.

One paragraph struck me as especially significant. She had written: "We have always tried to do right. We have gone to church. We have read our Bible. And every day we have said our prayers. Every night before going to bed we have said "Now I lay me down to sleep...."

Here was a person over seventy years of age—an active church worker—who had never gotten beyond the little prayer she had learned as a child. Somewhere along the line someone had slipped up. No wonder that in a crisis, like that of losing her husband, she did not know how to pray.

Prayer is to the spiritual man or woman what water and sunlight are to the flower. It is what material food is to the physical body. Just as the rose without water and the body without food weaken, wither, and die, so the soul of man weakens and withers without communion with God.

Man is a dual being: There is the physical body (the "... temple of the Holy Spirit..." I CORINTHIANS 6:19), in which one lives; And there is the spiritual element (that extra something which distinguishes man from the lower forms of animal creation). These elements are one, yet thy are two, each with its own requirements. In order to develop and be strong, each must be fed separately, and with its own kind of food. Man cannot really live with physical bread alone—prayer is as important to the spiritual man as bread is to the body.

Man has within him something of God. When he was

created, God ". . . breathed into his nostrils the breath of life
. . ." (GENESIS 2:7). In other words, God placed within man a
part of Himself, and man became different from all other of
God's creation.

The Psalmist was even more emphatic in defining man's
relationship to God. In Psalm 8 we are told that man was
made a ". . . little lower than God [Himself] . . ." (5, ASV) —
greater than anything else God did or created. God gave to
man His own image and likeness (spiritual, not physical, because God does not have a physical likeness). He gave to him
dominion and power, as well as the creative possibilities for
growth and development. The physical body of man is temporal, and will eventually return unto dust, from which it
came; but the spiritual being is of vastly more importance,
because it is eternal.

How mistakenly stupid man is when he gives so much attention to that which is temporal, but neglects that which is of
infinitely greater worth. How misguided he is when his heart
is melted by the thought of a physically hungry child, but is
unmoved and callous towards the spiritually hungry and
dying.

The God-qualities in man, just as the early stages of body
development, are in embryo—they must be cultivated, they
must be carefully nurtured, and they must remain in constant
touch with their Father-Creator in order to develop muscle
and sinew.

"Why should man pray?"

Man has to pray in order to survive spiritually. Through
prayer he receives spiritual nourishment without which he
will spiritually wither and die.

Through prayer—real, true prayer—he lives in the presence
of and has communion with the One toward whom he, by
nature, is supposed to be growing.

The soul hungers for fellowship with God. In the lives of

everyone there come those moments when, restless and tormented, we long to reach out and find something more substantial than that round about us. There come moments when we feel our feet sinking in the "quicksands" of an apparently meaningless and unsatisfactory life, and we wish to find a solid "rock" of confidence and assurance through which we can find hope and salvation. The Psalmist (PSALM 42:1,2) expressed this feeling beautifully: "As a hart longs for flowing streams, so longs my soul for thee, O God. My soul thirsts for God, for the living God...."

If these moments lead us to God in prayer, and we come to know the security and the confidence of lives wrapped up in him, we have learned to live. But if they do not do this, they are liable to lead us to frustration and despair.

The soul hungers for communion with God, just as the body hungers for physical food. And just as the body, if not fed, reaches a stage where hunger pangs are lost in weakness, so the soul, if not fed, becomes numb and less persistent in its longing for God.

Fellowship with God through prayer strengthens the whole man—it makes the impossible possible; it opens up "doors" to greater understanding of the things of God; it brightens the countenance and sweetens the whole life; it casts out fear and brings confidence and courage. A life spent in close communion with God becomes an attractive life.

I eat material food because my body needs it in order to be healthy and strong. I pray because my soul needs it in order to be healthy and strong—because there are so many things in life that can only be done if I live close to God.

Jesus spent much time in prayer. It is noteworthy that most of His greatest miracles were preceded or followed by all-night vigils with His Father, God. It is also noteworthy that the outstanding spiritual leaders of all time—those who have blazed the spiritual "trails" and moved the Kingdom of **God** forward—have been men and women of consecrated prayer.

I water my roses and give them sunshine because otherwise they would die. I nourish my soul through prayer because that is the only way it can flourish and be alive.

God loves us with a love so understanding and deep that He can have mercy on our weaknesses and forgive our transgressions. But He does not force Himself upon us. He shows us how intensely He loves us, how deep is His desire for our love, and how anxious He is to have fellowship with us; but if we turn our backs upon Him, He does not force His presence upon us.

The Parable of the Prodigal Son is a striking illustration of this. It must have cut deeply into the soul of the father when his youngest son came asking for his inheritance, and saying that he was tired of the home ties and of fatherly guidance, and that he wanted to go out into the world on his own. Doubtless, many times men have wondered why the father did not try to dissuade his son, or even refuse to give him his inheritance, in an effort to keep him at home. That would have been the human thing to do—that is the thing which you would have done, that is the thing I would have done. But Jesus was giving a lesson in the Fatherhood of God. He longs for our presence, and, if we stray, is ever ready to receive us back, but He does not compel us to continue in fellowship with Him.

We often say that God is "omnipresent"—in a certain sense that is very true, but in another sense it is not true. In deed, God is always present:

when He is needed (PHILIPPIANS 4:19);
when we call upon Him (PSALM 145:18);
when we are about His business (MATTHEW 28:20);
when we are in true prayer (MATTHEW 6:6).

But just as there can be no sound without an eardrum on which the sound waves can fall, so there can be no "presence of God" for the individual whose soul is closed against His presence.

The air about us is filled with music and with voices. If we have a radio or a television set we can pick them up; but unless we turn the instruments on and tune them properly, the music and the voices might just as well not exist—in fact, for us they would not exist.

The lives of too many, so-called Christians are anemic and unfruitful because they have neglected to open the "doors" of their minds and hearts, and permitted God to come in and speak to them.

Man must not only pray in order to have spiritual life—the character of his praying determines the quality and the strength of that life.

One cannot always reach a "mountaintop" of spiritual experience when he prays. There are different levels of accomplishment in prayer. We must not be discouraged if frequently we fail to get through to God, or if the level of our experience is not always the highest. But always we must strive to reach the highest.

Most of the time man lives on a midway plane of accomplishment intellectually, emotionally, and spiritually. But there come moments when he goes far beyond this and reaches a higher level. His ambition and his hope must always be for the highest. In prayer man may only occasionally reach that complete rapport with God. Some may reach it only once or twice in a lifetime, but when it does come, it so electrifies his whole life and being that it makes his Christian hold on God satisfyingly permanent and unshakable.

2. WHAT IS PRAYER?

THERE WAS A challenging sparkle in Susan's eyes as she spoke: "You have told us that we should pray; but what is prayer? What are we talking about when we talk about 'prayer'?"

Is it asking God for something we need or want, believing that He will give it to us? Is it meditation—the kind of meditation in which we strive to reach out and establish a rapport with God? Is it contemplation mingled with adoration, like when we stand watching the glories of a tropical sunset, and from that beauty let our thoughts reach on and on until we are swept into the ecstasies of a "seventh heaven"? Is it an earnest seeking after God, as when we lose ourselves in the study of His divine Word, and are able to see His face on the printed page and hear His voice open up to us the mysteries which a casual reading can but fail to reveal?

Can a sinner pray? Can an infidel pray? Will God hear their prayers and answer them as readily as He will those of a true believer? When they ask for things, will they get them as readily as will the saint of God?

These are questions as old as man himself.

Being of such vital importance—so big and comprehensive, and dealing with the spiritual relationship of man with God— no one can give a definition of "prayer." We can only define that which is smaller than we are, that which we are wise enough to understand.

We cannot define "God." If we could, He would not be God. We can name some of His attributes and some of the things He does; we can be thrilled by the immenseness and glory of His universe; we can tell how we feel in His presence. But that is about all. Our finite minds are so feeble, and our human understanding is so limited—that is why we have to accept God, and so many other things, like the trinity, the incarnation, and the bodily resurrection, on faith.

My feeble mind cannot understand "eternity." To me, everything has to have a beginning and an end. If eternity had a beginning, what was there before? If time is to end, what will there be afterwards?

Space scientists tell us that if a rocket could travel at the speed of light and travel in the same direction for a trillion years, its relative position with reference to the center of the universe would be exactly the same as when it started. My feeble mind cannot comprehend this; but I am compelled to accept it, because to believe the alternative would be a thousand times more difficult.

The person who denies all that he cannot understand is not an intellectual, but, rather, a presumptuous idiot.

I am more sure of the things I have to accept on faith than I am of the things I think I understand. The things I think I understand keep changing. Theories and so-called natural laws are in constant flux; and that which I think I know today is proven false tomorrow. But the things of God, which I accept on faith, are eternal, because God is eternal.

In the light of these things, how shall we go about trying to answer the question "What is prayer"? Perhaps the best way would be for us to let Jesus help us. While He never gave a direct definition of prayer, He did, in an indirect and perhaps in a better way, answer the question.

On one occasion, after one of his seasons of prayer, one of the disciples said to Him: "'... Lord, teach us to pray ...'" (LUKE 11:1).

Christ's followers were praying men. Being Jews, three times each day they repeated the Shema, with its eighteen petitions. They doubtless observed the other Jewish ceremonial prayers. Besides this, they had learned much from the example and teaching of Jesus. Yet they realized that there was something lacking. With him there was less formality, and an intimacy of spirit with God which they could not feel. As He prayed, His face must have glowed as did the face of Moses when he communed with God on Sinai. After a season of prayer there was about Him a greater sparkle and vitality.

I imagine they talked about this among themselves, and wondered. I can see John whispering to Peter as the Master came back to them from His all-night prayer vigil: "Look, Peter," he would say, "see how His face shines."

And Peter would answer: "Yes, John, I have noticed that, and somehow I feel smaller in His presence. It makes me want to run away, and yet I cannot. I feel unclean. And yet I have an overwhelming desire to know Him better, and have Him touch me, strip me of all my selfishness, and make me whole."

It was after one of these prayer vigils that the disciple (perhaps it was Peter or John) came with his petition: "Lord, teach us to pray." *Help us to find in prayer that which You find. Help us to shed the formality, and the sham of repetition. Help us to know God as You know Him, and to be able to commune with Him as You do.*

Matthew (MATTHEW 6:5-15) gives a much fuller account of the incident than Luke does. According to Matthew, Jesus laid down certain basic principles for prayer.

First: Do not make a show of it. Prayer is something intimate, like lovemaking. It loses its sacredness if paraded before men. The hypocrites liked to pray standing on the street corners or in the public buildings, so that they would be seen of men. Jesus said this is a "mockery." He said " '. . . When you pray, go into your room and shut the door and pray to your Father who is in secret; and your Father who sees in secret will reward you.' " (MATTHEW 6:6).

One of the things which has bothered me in my ministry has been the public prayers. So many times, and this especially when someone has said to me, "Reverend, that was such a beautiful prayer," I have felt ashamed and have wondered if I was unconsciously praying to the congregation, instead of to God. And I have felt like falling down on my knees and crying: "Forgive me, Lord."

The *second* principle laid down by Jesus is not to use a lot of words (MATTHEW 6:7). Prayer should be a time of listening, more than of talking. God knows what is in our hearts before we utter a word. In fact, God must sometimes want to shed a tear when He listens to the shallow words of our lips, and knows how completely they give the lie to that which is really in our hearts. Jesus said that we do not have to argue with God—we do not have to repeat things over and over in the hope that we can thus beat God down and get Him to do that which we wish, regardless of the fact that He had rather not do it.

He said that we do not have to explain things to God—He knows what our needs are before we ask a thing of Him. Some years ago I knew a woman—and a very consecrated woman, at that—who would not take medicine. She believed that God would heal her; but she went to the doctor to get her case diagnosed, so that she could tell God exactly what was wrong with her. Do not smile at this; because in her misguided faith, this poor woman was absolutely sincere. Instead of smiling, look deep into your own prayer life and see if perchance you are not guilty of something as mistaken and false.

Third: We do not have to occupy much time asking for "things," because God knows what we need before we ask Him, and He is always anxious to give to His children that which is best (MATTHEW 6:8). He never desires to withhold from His children that which is best for them. Too many people look upon God more as a rich and benevolent "uncle." When they want something, they are very solicitous, but when their wants have been supplied, they have very little time for God. They are like the little boy who, being asked if they prayed every day at his house, replied: "No, some days we don't need nuthin'."

A young prizefighter recently showed a great understanding of prayer. A reporter noted that this young man knelt in prayer just before the beginning of a fight. At the close of the fight the reporter asked the young fighter what he prayed for.

"First," said the lad, "I pray that it will be a clean fight. And second, I pray that no one gets hurt."

"But," asked the reporter, "do you not pray that you win?"

"No," said the fighter, "I never pray that I win. What if the other boy prays too. Then what is God going to do?"

The purpose of prayer is not to change God—to get Him to do something which He does not want to do. But, rather, it is to change us—to get ourselves in a condition so that we are able to receive that which God wants to give us. God's only limitation is that which we, through our lack of spiritual preparation, give Him.

The asking for things certainly has its place in prayer— although it may not be the most important part of prayer, it is nevertheless a very important part. It is natural for a child, when he gets his finger mashed, to run to mother for comfort. When he is hungry, it is natural for him to ask for something to eat. When he is lonesome, it is natural for him to seek companionship. I think God really appreciates His children coming to Him with their real needs, and talking them over with Him. Jesus, although His emphasis on prayer was quite different, did not frown upon the asking for things.

But there is a difference between asking mother for a piece of bread when we are hungry, and asking Santa Claus for a new red wagon when the one we got last year is abandoned out in the backyard with a broken wheel. There is a difference between asking father or mother for something because we love them, and know they love us, and asking a rich uncle for something, when the only time we ever think of him is when we want something. There is a difference between asking God at the end of a weary day for strength to make the last hard mile over the mountaintop, and asking Him in the dew of the morning to take the mountain away so that we will not have to climb it. There is a difference between asking for our daily bread, and asking for a banquet.

A woman came to me to get me to pray with her that her husband would get a better job. I found that he had held a better job, but had been demoted because of inefficiency. Another came and asked that we pray for a betterment in their financial affairs; the couple was just not able to provide proper food for their children, and they were deeply in debt. I found that the husband and wife together spent $30 a month for cigarettes. This $30 spent on food and other necessities would have about solved their financial problem.

Prayer for material things is most valuable many times in showing us the ridiculousness of our whole attitude towards prayer, and in helping us to get a truer and more spiritual concept of the nature of God. In both of the cases mentioned above, the women very readily saw the ridiculousness of their petitions. In the one case, both husband and wife stopped smoking; then, interestingly enough, through an unexpected source, their income increased, and they are now in better financial condition than they have ever been before. Without their praying for it, after they had done their part, God read the surrender in their hearts, and gave them far more than they could ever have asked.

The true test of prayer is not what it gets *for* us, but, rather, what it does *to* us.

Jesus laid down three principles to guide his followers in their prayer life. He gave to them and to us a model, or pattern, for praying. The three principles are:

Do not make a show of it.

Do not use a lot of words.

Do not be too concerned about things.

The prayer he gave is just a blueprint. He did not say: "When you pray, repeat this." He said: "After this manner, pray ye." I do not believe that Jesus ever intended that his prayer should ever become standardized, formalized, or ritualized. Sometimes I feel that Jesus must feel scandalized at the way his prayer is repeated or said in many religious services.

3. LORD, TEACH US TO PRAY

THE WORDS OF the Lord's Prayer can be repeated in 25 seconds. But to really pray it, with comprehension and meaning, requires hours. This prayer is but an outline—there are six guideposts, six great, directing principles. The bare words which Jesus gave are of little importance, but the great principles which underlie this prayer are of infinite importance. It is relatively unimportant what words we use. It is tragedy if we repeat the words and lose the basic, creative, eternal principles.

Perhaps the best way to understand the great privileges and opportunities of prayer; the best way to learn the attitudes, feelings, and understandings which we should bring to God as we approach Him in prayer; the best way to be prepared to talk with Him, and know what to request, is to spend a little time studying the model He gave His followers in reply to their request for instruction.

Before we start a study of this great prayer, it is wise to look at it as a whole. (We will use Matthew's account, and the King James translation: MATTHEW 6:9–13).

It is easy to picture the Master standing there, closely surrounded by his faithful followers (a deep sense of expectancy hovering over the small group), the light of day silently stealing away over the western horizon, the departing sun catching the tints of gold in His hair and beard, and the gentle winds picking up His mellow voice and carrying it out over the waters of the Red Sea:

> ... *Our Father which art in heaven, Hallowed be thy name. Thy kingdom come. Thy will be done in earth, as it is in heaven. Give us this day our daily bread. And forgive us our debts, as we forgive our debtors. And lead us not into temptation, but deliver us from evil: For thine is the kingdom, and the power, and the glory, for ever. Amen.*

The group must have been startled by the brevity of the prayer; they doubtless had expected a long dissertation. But this, in sixty-five simple words, was his lesson. Never has there been a more powerful combination of sixty-five words. Never has a more comprehensive, power-packed, thought-provoking statement been uttered.

I am sure that the disciples, just as we do today, failed to comprehend all that the Master was endeavoring to teach them. And I can imagine that on many occasions, as they rested in the evening in the Judean hills, they asked Him: "Lord, we still do not understand. Continue to teach us to pray."

And Jesus, taking the prayer principle by principle, doubtless continued to teach them.

Our Father which art in heaven. "Our Father," not "my" Father, but "our" Father. The first-person singular is not used in the whole prayer. There is not a selfish petition in it. God's Kingdom is a family. I am an individual, but I cannot live

41

alone. I cannot think of myself, or of my family, or of my community, or of my church, or of my nation, or of my race alone, and apart from the rest of the family of God. I am a part of a great whole. As Paul said in Romans 12:5 (KJV), we are all "one body in Christ," and "members one of another."

The first great lesson that accepting Christ should stamp indelibly on the hearts and minds of those who would follow Him is the Fatherhood of God and the brotherhood of man. In Christ, there is no Jew or Gentile, bond or free (I CORINTHIANS 12:13, KJV). We are all one body in Him. Until I can kneel by a black man, or an Indian, or a Chinese, and, forgetting his color and his station in life, sincerely pray "our Father," the full meaning of this prayer is not mine. Prejudice, envy, suspicion, and hate cannot exist in the same heart with a true, understanding love for God. Neither can a lack of interest in the welfare of the rest of mankind. Anyone who fails to accept every other child of God as his brother, or who builds a barrier between himself and any other man because of race, color, nationality, or social or economic condition, cannot in truth pray this prayer. And anyone who cannot in sincerity pray this prayer has tragically flunked Christ's first lesson in prayer, and is in grave danger of not being able to offer any prayer that will bring him very close to God.

Of course, anyone can ask God for things; anyone can pray if he thinks of prayer as the asking for material blessings. Rather, prayer should be a close communion with God—a complete throwing back of the "curtain" of selfishness and egotism, without reserve—such as: "Reveal Thyself to me, O God. Make me to know Thee, to understand Thee, to be more like Thee, that I may think Thy thoughts, live Thy way, and speak Thy words; that I may know in every crisis what to do; that when faced with a task I may be able to meet it in Thy way, with the assurance of Thy strength to help me; that when

I am tested and tried I may never falter or fail." If this be your idea of prayer—and it should be—then you cannot really pray until you are willing to accept every man as the child of God and as your brother—until you are interested in what happens to him, and are as anxious for him to have the best things of life as you are to have them yourself.

Jesus, when asked for the greatest commandment, must have startled his questioners by saying simply: ". . . love the Lord thy God . . ." and ". . . love thy neighbour as thyself." (MATTHEW 22:37–40, KJV). On these two commandments hinge everything else. How bitterly have men fought and divided over hair-splitting shades of theological doctrines. How tragic have been the heresy hunts. And how confused have been the hearts and minds of earnest souls caught up in the swells of church controversies. These things must have grieved the heart of God, and caused heaven to go into mourning.

Love God, and you will try to please Him; you will want to know more about His teaching; you will seek out His presence through meditation and prayer.

Love your fellowman as you do yourself and you will not, intentionally, cause him sorrow or pain; you will not defraud or mistreat him in any way; you will endeavor to understand instead of being suspicious; you will forgive his mistakes, and always be willing to reach out a helping hand when he needs a friend.

How different the history of the church would have been if its leaders had put first things first: "our Father," I love you, God; "my brother," I love you as myself.

He who cannot recognize and accept the brotherhood of man is denying the *Fatherhood* of God, and can scarcely, in sincerity, continue this prayer, because Jesus, by placing this at the very beginning, made it basic to the whole prayer.

Let us be conscious of our brother when we pray.

Hallowed be thy name. The first purpose of prayer is to praise God—to appreciate Him—to love and adore Him. There must be something of that feeling which the Psalmist had when he sang: "As the hart panteth after the water brooks, so panteth my soul after thee, O God. My soul thirsteth for God, for the living God . . ." (PSALM 42:1,2, KJV).

To too many people, God is a kind of Santa Claus, or even a "rich uncle"; Someone who supplies their needs; Someone to whom they can go when in trouble; Someone who can bind up their broken hearts. God is all of these, but He is also vastly more. He is our Father—we are made in His image; He created us just a little lower than Himself; and, above everything else, He asks for our love, our devotion, and our adoration.

The real purpose of prayer is to bring us into close communion with God. Jesus did not condemn the asking for things or personal favors, but He said that these are unimportant because God knows what we need before we ask; He intimated that if we come to God in prayer thinking of ourselves, or of those close by us; if we come thinking of the everyday affairs of life; if we come asking for material things or blessings which we desire, we are liable to find the circuit to God closed. It is not what prayer gets for us that counts—it is what prayer does to us. Its purpose is not to change God, but to change us.

Jesus said to come to prayer with an overshadowing desire to praise God—thinking on His greatness, remembering His loving kindness, standing in awe of His majesty, feeling the tenderness of His Fatherhood—come to Him with a "Hallelujah Chorus" of praise in your heart.

We tend to become like those we love—like those with whom we associate, talk, dream, and share creative hours of silence. A child becomes like his father, not when he comes running and asks for a dime or permission to do something, and then runs away, but when he comes tired, or discouraged, or just impelled by a desire for fellowship and companionship, and crawls up onto his father's lap, snuggles down in his father's arms, and, with love and devotion in his heart, says, "Daddy, tell me a story," or when he just lingers, overwhelmed with the consciousness of his father's love and goodness.

We become like our heavenly Father when we come to Him contemplating his wondrous greatness, realizing the all-embracing tenderness of his goodness and love. We become like Him when we come thinking, not of ourselves, but of Him; thinking, not of our needs, but of His goodness; desiring not to get something from Him, but, rather, desiring to give ourselves to Him, to be at one with Him.

Jesus said that true prayer begins with a longing for God; with a feeling of expansion, instead of contraction; with a desire to give Him our worship and love, instead of getting something from Him.

Did you ever watch two lovers sitting on a park bench, holding hands? Minutes, sometimes an hour, might pass without a word being spoken; they seem oblivious to the passing throng, or anything going on about them; they are happy just to be in each other's presence—words are not only superfluous, but would break the spell of communion.

Fortunate is the person who has reached the state of spiritual development where he can dwell on the "mountain peak" of this kind of communion with God. He then is able to pray truly: "Hallowed be thy name."

Thy kingdom come—Thy will be done in earth, as it is in heaven.—If we really know God—how marvelous He is, what

He can do for those who walk in daily communion with Him, and how lost mankind is without Him—our next petition will be: "Thy kingdom come—Thy will be done in earth, as it is in heaven." This will come automatically before we think of anything personal for ourselves.

Jesus said that he came into the world ". . . not to bring peace, but a sword" (MATTHEW 10:34, KJV). Jesus was not speaking of "war" in the sense we use the term; He was not speaking of material strife—Jesus hated that, and His whole teaching is in opposition to it; He was simply using material terms which the people would understand.

He said He did not come to bring peace—that is, contentment, complacency, satisfaction with the status quo. He came to stir men up—to shatter their self-satisfied, easy-going way of life. He came to stir them up—to make them discontent with that which was. He came to instill in them a consuming desire for a better way of life, and to give them the passion to pray for, to work for, and, if necessary, to die for the Cause which brought Him into the world—the Cause for which He was willing to die.

Jesus, contrary to the general impression, was not an easy-going, contented Man. He carried the burden of a lost world in His heart. Jesus never meant for man to be at peace with himself so long as there is one lost soul in this universe—so long as there is injustice, envy, jealousy, hatred, and greed.

When Jesus went into the mountains to pray—and He often spent entire nights out alone in the darkness with His heavenly Father—He must have been troubled in spirit. The immenseness of the task which brought Him into the world, the indifference of the people, the inability of His own disciples to understand the real nature of His Kingdom, the clamor for material things, and the seeming inability to comprehend spiritual values—these things must have pressed in on Him and made Him entreat His Father: "Thy kingdom come, O God; Thy will be done. Help me, O Father, to fulfill my mission. Use me. Let me die that the world may be saved."

Jesus taught His disciples out of His own experience, and He knew that anyone who enters through that portal of genuine worship, and comes to feel the presence of God, can but make his petition for the salvation of the world: "Thy kingdom come; Thy will be done." And he who prays this prayer must be willing to give himself that his petition be fulfilled.

Of course, there is a certain peace which comes with the acceptance of Christ as Saviour; but it is a peace like that at the center of a hurricane—a quiet confidence and faith—while all about rage the "howling winds" of concern for the homeless, the broken-hearted, the tempted, the weak, the spiritually blind, the selfish, and the lost.

To the one who has experienced the presence of God, and has really prayed "hallowed be Thy name," there is always present the disturbing challenge of the great commission— "Go therefore and make disciples of all nations" (MATTHEW 28:19). There is always the inability to take fully to self the fruits of the saving power of Christ's sacrifice and love as long as there are others in the world—our brothers—who have never had adequate opportunity to know and to enjoy that salvation and life.

The "peace-of-mind" cult has done a world of damage to the cause of Christ. Being unable to sleep is not always a tragedy—the *cause* of the loss of sleep *is* a tragedy for a multitude of people; but inability to sleep is not always a calamity. The ox or the sheep on the hillside can lie down to undisturbed sleep when its belly is full. But this is not possible for a person with the concerns of a chaotic world upon his shoulders. Would that more people could be so concerned about the "unsaved" condition of the millions of our brothers who do not know Christ that they could not sleep, so concerned that they would get up and do something greater than they have ever done before.

Too many of us are like the disciples, who slept while the Master went through the agonies of Gethsemane. Too many of us might have had "peace of mind" while our Saviour, in agony because of a lost world, prayed: ". . . and his sweat was as it were great drops of blood falling down to the ground" (LUKE 22:44, KJV). Jesus, in giving us this blueprint for prayer, was not giving us words to repeat—He was giving us the principle upon which a truly Christian life could be developed. Before we think of our own personal needs or material desires, we must have a consuming concern for the salvation of the world.

When Jesus gave to His followers His last commission, He attached a promise to it—that He would be with them always. He never promised to be with them under any other conditions.

I have often wondered if perhaps the reason why so many people find so little vital meaning in their religion, and why they feel a bleak barrenness when they attempt to pray, is that they have failed to learn that "Thy kingdom come; Thy will be done" must come before "give us this day our daily bread," "forgive us our debts," or "lead us not into temptation."

Sometimes when people pray for the little, petty things of life—material things, "children" of their own brains and their own selfish hearts—they receive what they request because God does answer prayers, and many times does give that which they ask, even though their thoughts and desires are selfish, narrow, petty, and blind. But even when they get what they request, this is not much compared to the real blessings of a close communion with God, which should be the main objective of prayer. If we are like the man whom Jesus mentioned who liked to pray long prayers on the street corners and in the synagogues in order to gain the praise of men, we might get a reward, but we would miss the greatest rewards of all—the mystical fellowship with God, the deep spiritual awakening, and the inspiration and strength—which come when we really live in His presence.

What would happen to the world if all Christians caught the full meaning of this prayer the Master gave us, and put it into practice? If we were all more concerned with the bringing of the world to Christ than we are with our own selfish desires, there would be ushered in a spiritual revolution which would indeed bring to pass the prophecy of the prophets, when men ". . . shall beat their swords into plowshares, and their spears into pruninghooks . . ." and when men learn war no more (ISAIAH 2:4 and MICAH 4:3, KJV).

Give us this day our daily bread.—This sentence is the only one in the entire prayer in which something material is mentioned. We must agree that "daily bread" is not very much for which to ask. In fact, this is more a petition for restraint in our desires for material things than it is for the gift of something.

"Give us this day our daily bread"—this is an appeal, not for a banquet at Sardi's or the Ritz-Carlton, but for just enough to satisfy the simple needs of daily life; not for food to be stored up for tomorrow, next year, or even the proverbial "rainy day," but for just the needs of today.

In depth, it means: "Lord, take away from me all material selfishness and greed; take away from me overall concern and anxiety for tomorrow; take away from me the blinding worries and cares about how I am going to provide for this physical body; help me to look at life in its true perspective, and to be able to evaluate all things in terms of their true relationship to God and the spiritual being He made me. Help me to put first things first in my thinking, so that I can seek ". . . first the kingdom of God, and his righteousness . . ." (MATTHEW 6:33, KJV).

Jesus did not condemn the possession of material goods; He only condemned the placing of them *first* in our thoughts and desires. Too many times a man's possessions become his master—they possess him instead of his possessing them, they enslave his thoughts, his affections, his actions, his life.

The Apostle John is supposed to have been a man of means; Jesus never condemned this in him. When Zacchaeus told Jesus that he was going to give one-half of his wealth to feed the poor, and that if he had defrauded anyone, he was going to restore him fourfold, Jesus did not condemn him for keeping the balance—and it was supposed to have been a goodly balance, for "he was rich" (LUKE 19:2–9, KJV).

True, He told the rich young ruler to sell all that he had, and give it away. Wealth to that young man was like a cancer eating away his soul, and a cancer has to be cut out. He loved his money more than he loved God—instead of putting the Kingdom of God first, he was putting his wealth first. In such a case, a radical operation is required. Anything that stands between a man and God must be sacrificed, be that an arm, an eye, wealth, or position.

The trouble with the rich farmer whom God called a "fool" was not that he possessed great wealth—his sin was in looking upon the wealth which God had given to him as a personal possession, to be used in his own selfish way. He failed to recognize that the possession of material wealth places a heavy burden of responsibility upon a man. This man, instead of saying: "God has been good to me; I will use this wealth to feed the hungry, to clothe the naked, to lift the load of injustice from the shoulders of the oppressed, to cooperate with

God in the building of a better world," he said to his soul: "Soul, thou hast much goods laid up for many years; take thine ease; eat, drink, and be merry" (LUKE 12:19, 20 KJV).

Man really owns nothing, not even the life he lives—it is not his, it is loaned to him. Material possessions are only ours as stewards. The only "treasures" we can really keep are the ones we store up in heaven.

A wealthy Kansas rancher was showing his new minister over his thousands of acres of land. He said: "Look to the west—as far as you can see, it is all mine; and also to the east, and the north, and the south."

The minister looked puzzled for a few seconds, and then asked, "Are you sure that you *own* all of this?"

The rancher said, "Of course I am. I bought it, and paid for it. I hold papers to prove that. Do you dare intimate that it is not mine?"

The minister replied, "Ask me that question one-hundred years from now."

In order to truly pray "Give us this day our daily bread," one must be willing to be stripped down to bare necessities; to "seek first the Kingdom of God, and His righteousness" (MATTHEW 6:33, KJV) ; to make material things truly seecondary in his thoughts and desires. If these conditions are met, the presence or the absence of material wealth cannot affect his spiritual growth.

It is interesting to observe how the loss of wealth affected different people following the depression of the early thirties. Only one who has gone through it can realize what it means to go to bed a millionaire and wake up the next morning dispossessed of everything. Under the strain, many committed suicide, but many others found God. One man said: "When I was rich I did not have time for my family; I did not have time for my church; I did not have time for God. Looking after my money kept me busy 24 hours out of every day, including Sunday. Now with those worries taken away, I have really started to live."

"Give us this day our daily bread" could well be written for those of us who live in this modern world of tension, rivalry, and false standards of values, as: "Take us out from under the yoke of worry and concern about the merely physical things of life. Help us to be content with the minimum, and if perchance abundance be given us, help us to look upon it as a trust to be administered, not in a selfish way, but with love, and in the spirit of Jesus Christ."

Forgive us our debts, as we forgive our debtors.—This is one of the most explosive requests man can possibly make. If God failed to hear this plea without a tincture of His limitless understanding, love, and mercy, the gates of heaven might as well be closed, for none of us would ever be able to enter.

So often we hear supposedly Christian people say, "I can never forgive that," or, "I may forgive, but I can never forget," which means merely "lip" forgiveness, without the mind or the heart.

Too often we see people who carry grudges, or envy, or suspicion, or hate. We even see "church" people who will not speak to each other—sometimes they are elders or deacons. We see people, supposedly Christian, who quit going to church because someone hurt their feelings; they say, "I can never work or worship with that person again." We see people form factions, or cliques, within the congregation. If one faction makes a suggestion, the other will oppose it, not because it is bad, but because it was suggested by the wrong party. We see those same people stand up on Lord's Day morning and repeat, "Forgive us our debts, as we forgive our debtors." What would happen if God really took them at their word.

"Forgiveness" is one of the most difficult virtues to cultivate —it is difficult because in order to forgive, we must humble ourselves. If someone has mistreated us—or we think they have—our pride and dignity are injured. The animal within us cries out: "No one can do that to me, and get away with it." We harbor the hurt in our minds and keep turning it over in our hearts. Even when we want to forgive, we cannot do it alone—that is why Jesus included this petition in His prayer; that is why we should linger over it, and when we pray give God time to enter into our inner being, and give us the strength we need. The "law of the jungle" is strong within us. It says, "an eye for an eye, a tooth for a tooth." It takes a lot of the presence of God to make us "turn the other cheek," to "go the second mile," to pray for those who do us wrong, to love our enemies; but we never learn to live truly until we do exactly this. "Forgiveness" means that we wipe the "page" clean—like the father of the prodigal son, we restore the "garment" of respect and the "ring" of confidence; we hold no grudge or resentment. This attitude is difficult, but certainly not impossible to achieve. We need the help of God, but with that all things are possible through Christ, who strengthens us (PHILIPPIANS 4:13).

We do for our brother what we want God to do for us when we offend or disobey Him. Jesus had a good deal to say about forgiveness, but no place does he put it so dramatically or so dynamically as in this prayer. It is doubtful whether one can pray this prayer or, for that matter, any prayer that gets beyond the sound of his voice until he has done his best to be at peace with his brother.

God can only forgive those who have forgiveness in their own hearts. Can you imagine a heaven filled with unforgiving people—people whose hearts and minds are filled with envy, jealousy, back-biting, and hate? Can you imagine a heaven—

no matter where or what it is—that is broken up into factions and warring cliques? Can you think of a continuing life filled with unforgiving spirits as being anything other than hell?

It should be easy to see why it is impossible for God to forgive us unless we have the spirit of forgiveness in our hearts. Jesus showed us what it is to forgive—to the betraying Judas He offered His cheek; to the arresting soldier He restored an ear; to the vacillating, pusillanimous weakling in the judge's chair He gave kindness; to a frightened Peter, who had just finished cursing and declaring that he had never known Jesus, there was but a smile of pardon.

Far greater than any of these examples was His ultimate gift on the cross. Without the cross and the willing giving of Himself, His lesson of forgiveness would have been incomplete, and His work of salvation unfinished. When in the torment of crucifixion Jesus thought, not of Himself, but of His tormentors, and when He cried out to God, ". . . Father, forgive them, for they know not what they do . . ." (LUKE 23:34, KJV), He hung a hallowed "wreath of glory" about the forgiving heart, and opened a "door" to the everlasting presence of God. This door can never be closed to the one who forgives as he would desire to be forgiven.

Lead us not into temptation, but deliver us from evil.—God does not lead anyone into "temptation" in the sense in which we understand the word today. The idea here is, "Do not let us be overcome by temptation. When it approaches us, give us the strength to meet it head on, and fight our way through it."

Jesus did not tell us to ask that temptation be taken away from us. Although many times we feel that we would appreciate never being tempted, we know that temptation is a necessary result of being free. Were there no opportunity to disobey, there would be no virtue in obeying. Were it not possible to hate, there would be no virtue in loving.

Many times people ask: "Why did God, if He knew all things, permit Adam and Eve to be tempted?" or "Why did He not make them strong enough so that they could not disobey Him?" These are natural questions, and one should not feel ashamed to ask them; but they are illogical questions.

The only way God could have made man impervious to temptation and sin would have been to make him a machine, incapable of free choice.

We must remember that man is made a ". . . little lower than God [Himself] . . ." (PSALM 8:5, ASV), and is "crowned" by his Creator with glory and honor. Man is not only the highest creation of God, but he is the greatest God could produce; He has within him something of God Himself; He is made a little lower than God. In the story of creation, we are told that after man was formed from the dust of the earth (GENESIS 2:7, KJV) God ". . . breathed into his nostrils the breath of life; and man became a living soul." In other words, God placed a part of Himself in man—man is made in the image and likeness of God. That kind of man cannot be a machine.

Unless there are dual or multiple choices, there can be no free will. Unless man can deny God, there is no opportunity to accept Him. In other words, unless a man can sin, there is for him no righteousness—he is not a man at all, but a machine, and a machine cannot be in the image and likeness of God.

Even Jesus was tempted, not just in the wilderness, but in many other ways during His ministry on earth. As He stood that day at the parting of the ways, on His last trip to Jerusalem, He must have been tempted to take the easy way. One road led to Nazareth, the home of His boyhood days. Memories of its peacefully sloping hills; the tranquility of the shepherds tending their flocks; the lazy movements of the sheep;

and the dreamy tinkling of the camel bells as caravans moved slowly through the peaceful streets, must have awakened deep longings within Him. He must have remembered the happy moments with His mother—the songs she sang to Him, the prayers she taught him, the stories she told. He remembered Joseph, and the companionship He had with him in the workshop; how in the evenings, tired from the work of the day, they would sit out under the heavens and talk about the things of His heavenly Father. He must have had a flickering longing for the return of that peace and quiet, and a temptation to take that road instead of the other.

The other road led to Jerusalem, with its shame and hypocrisy—the city where men had converted His Father's "house of prayer" into a den of thieves. He knew that at the end of that road lay the lonely hour when even His most trusted followers would forsake Him, when a crown of thorns would be pressed upon His brow, and men would spit in His face. He knew that at the end of that road lay Calvary, with its agonies of crucifixion. Yes, for a moment He must have been tempted to take the easy road, but the temptation here, as in the wilderness, was but for a moment. With resolution He "steadfastly set his face to go to Jerusalem" (LUKE 9:51, KJV).

He was tempted in the Garden of Gethsemane, and even prayed that, if possible, "that cup of agony, that cup of death" on the cross might be spared Him. The temptation was but for a moment. There was a real struggle—a struggle that brought sweat like "great drops of blood" to His brow. The battle was soon over; and I can imagine that, with a smile of determination and victory on His face, He added: "not my will, but Thine be done."

If Jesus was tempted, how can we even dream of being spared? Why should we complain? Exercise makes us strong—our physical muscles become strong and hard only when we use them; without physical work we would become physical weaklings, and easy prey to every death-dealing germ with which we come in contact. The tree that stands near the ocean, where it is cruelly buffeted by mighty storms, may be gnarled and unsymmetrical in shape, but it sends its roots deep down, and with thousands of fingers maintains an unbreakable hold upon the earth.

God does not tempt anyone; neither does He keep temptation away from us. He lets us meet the trials and the testings. He wants us to be worthy of His image and likeness. He wants us to wear, with dignity and satisfaction, the glory and honor with which He "crowns" us. He wants us to be a credit to Him. He understands all of our weaknesses, but, like a good father, He does not shield us from the testings of life.

But neither does He leave us alone. He says: "I am always close by. I will strengthen and keep you. I will not stand by and see you tempted beyond what you can bear. You can always draw upon My strength. You must use the tools you have. You must fight with all your strength, but never be discouraged; like the lifesaver which the lifeguard throws out, I am always within your reach."

"Lead us not into temptation" really means: "Be always near, and make us conscious of Your presence, so that we will never lack either the courage to face the battle nor faith that the victory can be won."

One of the biggest temptations which has stalked me most of my life concerns the desire for quiet and peace. I have had a constantly haunting temptation to run away from the conflicts, turmoils, and unpleasant things of life. It would not have been difficult for me to become a hermit, hiding away in some isolated spot, and spending my days in contemplation and adoration.

Instead of permitting me to do that, God has placed me in

the thick of the "battle" of life. As a missionary for 33 years in South America and Puerto Rico, I seemed to have inherited a superabundance of problems and crises. As a minister, especially during the last eighteen years, I have been destined to serve small churches with special needs and challenging opportunities. Somehow I feel that God deliberately placed me in these positions. He wanted me to meet my temptation, overcome it, and, through exercise, stimulate and develop my soul. He did not want my life wasted in an easy, "do-nothing" existence, and He never failed to lead me and to give me the courage, strength, and determination which was needed.

Temptations come—God does not keep them away, but He gives us the strength to overcome them.

Let's review briefly the observations we have made about the skeleton prayer given by the Master in answer to those who requested: "Lord, teach us to pray."

First: We must remember that real prayer does not consist of the words which fall from our lips, but, rather, it is the deep longing which we carry in our hearts. In fact, none of us knows what to ask for. God knows much better than we do, not only what we need, but what we really want. It is related that the mother of St. Augustine prayed through an entire night in a chapel by the seashore for God to keep her son at home, where she hoped his soul might be saved. While she was on her knees, Augustine was boarding a ship for Italy. In Italy he met the saintly Ambrose, through whom he was converted. What his mother prayed for was denied; what she really wanted she got.

Second: Prayer is a communion. It is drawing close to God. It is letting our spirit meet its parent, the great spirit of God, and be filled and enlivened through that fellowship. It is letting the mind of God be in us, the strength of God flow through us. For this reason, the first essential element of prayer is adoration and worship: "Our Father . . . Hallowed be thy name. Thy kingdom come. . . ." Then we are prepared to receive and use the strength He gives us to earn our daily bread, to forgive our brother, to overcome temptation.

Third: Prayers are not to be "said"—they are to be lived. In I Thessalonians 5:17 (RSV) we are told "pray constantly," or without ceasing. This does not mean to stay on our knees all day. It means to make our whole life a prayer—a recognition of the greatness, goodness, and Fatherhood of God—and strive to live in constant harmony with Him. But we cannot live in harmony with God unless we know Him, and know His will for mankind. Therefore, an earnest, unprejudiced, prayerful study of the Bible is an essential part of our living. Not only through the Bible do we learn of God, but also through an unbiased study of the way He works in His universe, through the manifestation of His personality in the orderliness of day and night, of seedtime and harvest, of sunshine and rain, can we come to know and appreciate Him. We can see Him, too, in the lives of men and women—in the innocence of a newborn babe, in the faith and courage of a man who picks up a "mountain" and places it in the sea, and in the victorious smile of an octogenarian who has served his God well, and moves forward to receive his reward.

4. WHATSOEVER YOU ASK IN HIS NAME

ON ONE OCCASION Jesus said to His followers: "Whatever you ask in my name, I will do it . . ." (JOHN 14:13). This is perhaps one of the most misunderstood passages in the entire Bible. What do you think Jesus meant by this statement?

Certainly no reasonable person would pretend to believe that simply by adding these words to the end of a prayer—"in the name of Jesus"—he will get anything he asks. Such an addition is not a magic formula—a kind of "Aladdin's lamp"—which automatically opens the doors of heaven and causes God to grant a request, no matter how silly, selfish, or unwise it might be. Yet there are millions of people who, for practical purposes, teach and practice this kind of interpretation—if you want a new automobile, ask for it in the name of Jesus; if you want a different job, if you want to sell a piece of property or to pass an examination, or if you want to have someone brought to Christ or have a sick person healed, just ask for it in the name of Jesus.

Exactly what did Jesus mean when He said: "Whatever you ask in my name, I will do it . . ."? In order to find a true answer, it is necessary to study the whole prayer life of the Master—His words and His example.

Jesus prayed often, but we know very little of what He said in His prayers; in fact, it is doubtful that He used many words. With the exception of the prayer recorded in John 17—and that is not a long prayer—His prayers are noted for their brevity. The nights that He spent alone in the mountains were not spent in asking for things; in fact, so far as we know, with the exception of the prayer at Gethsemane, Jesus never asked for a personal thing.

The night vigils of the Master were doubtless spent in close spiritual communion with His Father, God—they were hours of agony and deep longing; hours of uncertainty and fatigue; they were hours of refreshment and renewal of strength (His greatest miracles came just after or just before an all-night vigil with God). I doubt that Jesus ever asked for an easy way or for a material object. His concern was, not for things, but for spiritual power, that the task for which He came into the world might be accomplished—that He might not fail either God or man.

In that longest and most dramatic, recorded prayer of Jesus (JOHN 17) we find that the burden of the prayer was for His followers—those of that day, and those who would come after them. We find that His concern was for the redemption of the world. He was concerned for the unity of His church—that His followers might be one, in the same sense that He and the Father are one—and the purpose for this was, not His own glory, but that the world might believe and be saved. There is not a single material request in the entire prayer.

When we study the life and the overall teachings of the Master, we find that He endeavored to get the desires and the concerns of man away from over-anxiety about material needs, and center them instead on the spiritual oneness of man with God. It is difficult for us to understand fully or appreciate His message in Matthew 6:19–34, but as we come to know Him more intimately, we must accept that this message is fundamental to all of His teachings. He did not deny our need for material things—He did not indicate that we are to fail to work for them. He said that there is something more important—that the best way to get the material things of life is to put them in a secondary, not a primary, place in our thoughts and our desires. He said: ". . . seek first his kingdom and his righteousness . . ." and all of the other things will come more easily (MATTHEW 6:33).

Jesus was a revolutionary. The religious leaders of His day had made of religion a ritual, a form, a soulless compliance with law. Instead of transforming the society about them, they had conformed, to a large degree, to the philosophy of their day. There was the feeling that an individual had to look first after himself. Fasting, reciting long prayers, paying tithes, looking pious, washing the hands before eating, offering sacrifices at stated times—these formal acts were considered as most important. Complying with them made a man religious. This had become their religion; when they complied with these rules, they felt that their duty had been performed and that they could follow their own selfish ways.

Jesus taught a way of life at the other extreme. In consequence, He was considered a subversive, and was crucified. If He lived today, He would be considered a destructive heretic by some, and a dangerous subversive by others.

Jesus brought a religion based on love. He said to love the Lord God with all our hearts, with all our souls, and with all our minds, and to love our neighbors as we do ourselves. He said further that on these two commandments all of the law and the prophets have their foundation (MATTHEW 22:35—40). He claimed to give only one new commandment—". . . that you love one another; even as I have loved you, that you also love one another" (JOHN 13:34).

Jesus taught that God is love, and that we must love one another if we are to be like Him. With Him, all jealousy, envy, suspicion, and hate are destructive of the God-directed and -sustained life. He taught that we are to be peace-makers, humble, merciful, and pure in heart, and that we are to do more than just "our part." Halfway was not enough for Jesus. In order to build a world brotherhood, in order to bring out the best in others as well as in ourselves, if compelled to go one mile, we are to go two, and if struck on one cheek, we are to turn the other (MATTHEW 5:38–42). In other words, we are not to be sticklers for "our rights." We are not to do just "our duty" (until one has done more than his duty, he has not done anything to merit credit). Instead, we are to try to understand our fellowman, even our enemies, and, by loving them, convert them into friends.

Jesus taught that "God is spirit," and that He must be worshipped "in spirit and truth" (JOHN 4:24). The place of worship does not matter; the form of worship is not important —the important thing is that we recognize the real nature of God and our essential relationship to Him, and that we cultivate that relationship. Outward signs can be deceiving; it is what is inside our hearts that counts. We do not have to actually shed the blood of our brother in order to be guilty of murder; we do not have to lay hands on a woman in order to commit adultery (MATTHEW 5:21, 22, 27, 28). Anyone can strictly comply with the laws concerning sacrifice, offer long prayers in the temple, pay tithes, and still not worship God.

True worship is an intimate and a precious thing—it is a personal relationship between God and human being. It is an at-oneness, a "love-feast," an experience in which adoration, awe, consuming desire for fellowship, and love of the worshipper for his God are recompensed by the consciousness of God being present, and God, not only revealing Himself, but giving Himself in an intimate communion, in which strength and guidance pass from Creator to child.

This teaching of Jesus makes it easier to understand what He meant when He said: "Whatever you ask in my name, I will do it. . . ." If we discard the thesis that He gave these words as a kind of magic, which would produce certain results, the alternative is readily understandable.

Was He not really saying: "If you understand Me and what I stand for, if you understand My relationship with the heavenly Father, if you have the same mind in you that I have in Me, if your relationship with your fellowman is the same as Mine, then you will know how to make requests of 'Our' Father who is in heaven, and whatever you ask will be granted unto you. And, even more than that, you will not only know how to make requests, and God will not only grant your requests, but you will know how to profit by what He gives to you."

To the degree that one is "at-one" with God, he can do anything that he desires. If he is in complete fellowship with God, anything that he may want to do will be right. Jesus was really saying: "Be at one with Me, and then anything that you may ask will be so completely in harmony with God's purpose and will that it will be done for you."

The kind of prayer which Jesus practiced and taught is not just a rushing to God with a hurried petition for something which we think we want. It is, rather, a dwelling in the presence of God and a transformation into His image and likeness. Its purpose is, not to get God to do something which He does not want to do, but, rather, a surrendering of ourselves to the will of God, so that He can do that which He wants to do. It is not a matter of what prayer gets for us, but, rather, what prayer does to us.

In I John 5:14, 15 we find these words: ". . . if we ask anything according to his will he hears us. And if we know that he hears us in whatever we ask, we know that we have obtained the requests made of him." In other words, the success of a prayer depends upon the success of getting through to God—being so in tune with Him that He hears the prayer.

God pays very little, if any, attention to our words. He looks deep into our souls, and reads what He finds there. He is always very conscious of our needs, and He is anxious to give to us that which is best for us. The moment we get through to Him (and that depends on us, not on God), which is important, not so much in order that He may hear us, but much more so that we can hear Him, we have nothing further about which to be concerned.

True prayer is not a ritual; it is not the use of a magic formula—it is the deep longing of a human being for communion with his Creator, God; it is a recognition of his dependence on God, and a sincere thanksgiving for all of the blessings which he has received.

I remember a critical time in 1942 in Puerto Rico. On faith, we had gone ahead with the starting of a new church in San Juan—we had started it six months previously without a single penny of guaranteed support for it; we had brought in one of our finest young ministers; we had signed an option to buy a lovely piece of property for $11,000. It was a propitious beginning.

Then World War II began. Money was hard to get; the price of property soared. The seller of the property was anxious to get out of her bargain because then she could get a higher price. If we lost that property, there was none other available in the area where we felt the church should be. Unless we produced $11,000 in thirty days, our option would not be worth the paper it was written on—and we had not a single penny.

We called our ministers together for a day of prayer. There

was something unique about the prayers that day—not one person prayed for $11,000. The burden of every prayer was: "Lord, You have brought us this far. We thank You for what You have done. We thought You wanted this church. We still think so. But unless You help us, it is going to be lost. Now, Lord, You tell us what to do, and we will try to do it. If You want us to fail, it is all right with us. If You want us to succeed, just tell us what to do, give us the strength and the courage, and we will try to do it. No matter what happens, God, You are our God, and we know that You do all things well."

Before the 30 days were up we had the $11,000, and that church has gone on to become, not only one of our strongest on the Island, but one of the most influential forces for moral and spiritual strength in that entire city of three-quarters of a million people.

True prayer is surrender to God; a confession of our weaknesses and sins; a longing to have His spirit dwell within us, a willingness to be used by Him in taking the message of Christ to all the world; a restless concern for other people, their hunger and thirst, both physical and spiritual. It is the giving of self to God, that He may dominate and control our complete beings. When we pray with this approach, we have really prayed, and whatever we may ask in His name will be done.

5. PRAYER FOR THE SICK

THERE IS SO much that we do not understand about prayer. Why is it that sometimes we get what we ask for, and other times we don't? This is especially true with reference to the healing of the sick.

Some years ago I was called by the daughter of an elderly lady who was dying of a heart condition. There were two doctors in attendance. They had given her every heart-stimulant possible. At last they said: "There is nothing more we can do. It is just a matter of minutes or hours." Only with the stethoscope could they distinguish any heartbeat; it was so long between breaths that they thought each one would be the last. At last (about 4 a.m.) the daughter asked me to go in and pray with her.

I asked everyone to leave the room; I placed one hand on her forehead, and with the other held one of her little, almost lifeless hands. I did not pray that God would heal her, but that He would be there with her, that He would place His hands upon her, and that He would cause His strength to flow into her frail little body. I asked Him to be present and take charge.

Shortly after this I went home, leaving instructions with the family to call me instantly if there was any change. Having been up all night, I fell asleep, and did not awaken until 9 o'clock. A bit ashamed of myself, I dressed and went hurriedly to her house. The daughter met me at the door, with a finger at her lips, signifying silence. When I reached the bedroom door and looked in, I saw the frail, little lady sitting up in bed taking toast and tea.

An interesting sidelight is that she did not remember any of the commotion which had gone on about her the night before —she did not remember the doctors being there, she did not remember the many times the needle had punctured her arm —but she did remember my hand upon her forehead, and she remembered the prayer. She was convinced that she had been healed through prayer, and I believe she was.

For three years after that she enjoyed health as good as she had for many years. Then she fell and broke her hip; she was in the hospital for eight weeks before she passed away. Now the baffling, difficult-to-explain thing is why she was healed the first time, but not the second. The second time we prayed just as earnestly and with, if possible, more faith than the first time, but, instead of getting well, she died. Why? I have found no one who can give a satisfactory answer.

A friend of mine is known far and wide as a "healer." He travels up and down the land, speaking about prayer and healing the sick. In his records are many cases of healing, some of them brought back from the very brink of death. I have no doubt that these are authentic cases, and I firmly believe that many of them would not have recovered had it not been for prayer.

In spite of this man's success as a healer, his wife—a true saint of God—died of cancer. People all over the United States prayed for her; some of them, tried and true saints of the

Lord, gave assurance that she would recover. Yet she grew steadily worse and died. Why?

There is so little we know about healing through prayer—Divine healing, spiritual healing, or whatever you care to call it. The great number and variety of healers—professional and amateur—greatly complicate the situation, and leave the ordinary Christian who believes in prayer and God's intervention in the healing of the sick greatly confused. They all attest to a long list of successful healings. So do the medicine men of Africa, the practitioners of voodoo in Haiti, the mental healers, and even the out-and-out charlatans.

The human body is so little understood—not even the physicians know all there is to be known about it. We do know that God has built into the body a myriad of monitors to warn us of danger—pain is just a warning signal, fever is to tell us that there are poisons in the system. God has also built in a number of corrective forces—bodily functions which spring into action when danger approaches. Constantly there is a battle going on in our bodies—enemy germs are constantly fighting to gain control, but the healthy body is able to throw them off. All of us, at one time or another, have harbored the germs of tuberculosis, but if we were healthy and strong, we were able to overcome them without ever knowing they were there. It is only when the "enemy" becomes too strong for the normal bodily resistance that we get sick, and have to call the doctor. The doctor's medicine does not heal us—it just reinforces the lifeguards which God has placed in the body, and enables them to win the battle.

Medicine alone is not sufficient—the will to get well is much more potent than medicine, and surrender to death has taken many people earlier than necessary to their graves. Fear tends to paralyze the proper functioning of the body—pessimism destroys the will to fight, discouragement reduces resistance, and envy, jealousy, and hate disturb the proper balance in bodily functions, and leave one a prey to destructive forces within. Here a witch doctor, a mental healer, or a charlatan may be able to effect a cure simply by restoring the patient's desire to live, his confidence, and his willingness to fight.

There are times when medicine is not sufficient, and when more than a positive mental attitude is required—there are times when only a great faith founded in Someone greater than self, greater than doctors, and greater than relatives and friends is required; there are times when only the One who created our bodies, the One who knows all of its mysteries and holds all of its secrets in His heart, can heal its wounds.

A prominent doctor was once asked what was most important in his preparation for a medical career. In reply he stated: "You know, if I am to be a good surgeon, a good doctor, I must know three subjects—physiology, mental therapeutics, and religion." When he was asked why religion was important, he replied: "Because the body and the soul live so close together that they catch each other's diseases. When I go into a sick room, I have to realize that sometimes man needs a promise more than he needs a pill. And before I can cure the fever, I must quench the fear that is causing the fever."

Dr. Sladen of the Ford Hospital in Detroit, one of the greatest contemporary men of medicine, in addressing the Convention of American Surgeons meeting in Pittsburgh some years ago, made the following statement: "Gentlemen, in medicine, you and I must need, in a day like this when men are cracking up all about us, something more than can be bought in the corner drugstore. We need a great grip on God."

It is interesting that psychiatry is turning more and more toward religion—the psychiatrist's couch is only a step away from prayer—the complete relaxation, the relinquishing of the idea that "I have to do it all myself," the placing of self in some other hands, and the faith that help can and will come.

Many psychiatrists—and these the ones whose success is most pronounced—recognize that the surest, and in many cases the only, way to help people, especially those over forty, is to help them find a more solid and secure religious foundation for their lives. In many cases they recommend a steady, consistent prayer life for their patients.

In my ministry of sixty years, I have seen scores of instances where God intervened in the healing of sick bodies and minds, and in some cases brought them back from close to death.

There is the case of the young man I was called to see late one stormy night—his doctor had called me, and when I arrived was waiting in the hall outside the hospital room. He said: "Reverend, unless you can do something, that man is going to die. And the strange thing is he does not need to die. I have done everything I know, but he does not respond to medical treatment. There is something 'eating' at his soul, and that something is making him desperately sick. From now on it is up to you and God. I will be praying for you."

When I went into the room, the young man was in a coma. I knew it was useless to try to talk with him, so I sat by the bed and started to read from the Bible. I also read from a little, personal manual which I use in the sickroom, one section of which has all of the love-passages grouped together. I read the Sermon on the Mount, and then I read the love-passages again. When I had finished, the eyelids flickered, as though the eyes would open. For half an hour I sat there in silent prayer. Then I talked to myself, but in an audible voice, about the goodness of God, and how anxious He is to strengthen and help us. I do not know whether the patient heard a single word I said or not. Two hours later, when the doctor returned, he said: "The crisis has passed. He will live."

I would not attempt to try to explain the reversal. But this I know—God had been present, and had, in His way, gathered up the frayed ends of the "thread" of life which was rapidly giving way and tied them together again.

Another case is that of a fine Christian woman who suffered from a heart condition. Many times she had been at the brink of death, and had rallied. I remember one such occasion—not only was her heart acting up, but she had a congestion of the lungs. The doctor pronounced her condition "critical." Her son called me, and I went to visit and pray with her. We both prayed, and then I just sat in the room in deep meditation and silent prayer. Within a few minutes she fell asleep; her breathing became normal; a relaxed expression came over her face; and all evidences of pain were gone.

When the doctor arrived that afternoon, he was startled to find that the congestion had disappeared from her lungs, and her heart was close to normal. He pronounced her out of danger and in better condition than she had been for some time.

What had happened? All I know is that God had been there, and that in some way—His way—He had placed His healing hands upon her. I know that I had nothing to do with her recovery, except, perhaps, that by joining my prayers with hers the "floodgates" of God's healing power were opened so that strength could flow into her body.

Why does God permit anyone to be ill? To die? Why does He not heal every illness? I do not know. He could if He wanted to—if there was a reason for it. He could cause a new leg to grow for that cripple who has lost his; He could restore the vital organ completely destroyed by cancer; He could heal a heart through which a bullet has passed—He can do anything He wants to. If I understood all of the mysteries of infinite wisdom, I would know why He does some things and does not do others. But I do not possess this perfect knowledge; only God Himself has that. For this reason, it is not for me to question His ways or to doubt His wisdom and love.

I, who cannot understand how a star is held in its place or how a flower can come from a tiny seed, am not going to question the wisdom and the love of He who made the stars and flung them out over the endless expanse of space, and sweetened the air about us with the delicate perfume of the violet and the rose.

God does not always answer our prayers in the same way. At times, we may not even recognize the answer to our prayers for the sick.

One of the most triumphant souls I have ever known was a sweet-faced, little woman who had been bedfast for eight years. She could not move a hand or a foot; she could not turn her head. She could turn her eyes, and O, what depth of spiritual sparkle and glow they possessed. She had not been off her bed, except when she was lifted, for eight years. But she was one of the most radiant Christians I have ever known.

When, as pastor of her church, I first went to call on her, it was with fear and trembling. I said to myself: "What can I say to this poor soul? What can I do to cheer her a bit? How can I make her more content with her lot?" I had been by her bedside but a few seconds before I realized that I was the "poor soul"; that I was the one who needed cheering up; that she was the stronger of the two, and that I was on the receiving end of the line.

We talked a while. She told me that at first she had been rebellious and resentful; that for a time she could not really pray. Then, gradually, God came through to her, and had transformed her life.

We prayed together—I prayed and she prayed. Later, as I compared the two prayers, I was ashamed of my feeble effort. For days afterward my principal prayer was "Lord, teach me to pray."

In her prayer she did not ask God to heal her; she did not ask Him to ease her pain—and at the time she was in great pain; she just talked to Him as though He were sitting there by her bedside; she thanked Him for the many blessings He was giving to her (at the time I could see very few blessings, but later I learned to recognize them); but mostly she thanked Him for His presence with her, and for the sweet communion they had together.

I realized that she had learned the secret of real prayer—intimate, personal communion with God. I wondered if God had not really given to her the best possible answer to any prayer—a spirit-filled life, instead of a healed physical body.

The lady to whom I referred earlier—the one who astonished her doctors by miraculously recovering, almost instantaneously, from a lung congestion—went to sleep one night and quietly slipped away into the heavenly presence of her God. Who can say that her prayer and the prayers of her family and friends were not answered?

God holds our lives in His hands. He made our bodies and gave them every fiber and tissue, every heartbeat, and every brain reaction. He established the "laws" by which our bodies function, and it is only through Him that life is sustained.

We know that the spirit within us is part of God; that we are made just a "little less than God," and crowned by Him "with glory and honor" (PSALM 8:5). We know that we bear His image and likeness, and that He so loved us that He gave His only begotten Son that we might have life and have it more abundantly (JOHN 3:16). We know that God cannot be indifferent to those upon whom He has lavished so much of

Himself, and we know that whenever we recommend anyone, sick or well, to Him in prayer, He will not be unsympathetic to our petition, and both we and the one for whom we pray will be blessed.

If that blessing results in the healing of the sick one, wonderful and good. If it does not result in the physical healing of the body, but helps the person to be better prepared to enter into that eternal mansion which Jesus said He went to prepare, then, also, well and good. After all, the greatest thing is not the healing of the physical body, important as that may be to us, but, rather, it is that we be more completely committed to God, and that, in His infallible wisdom, His will be done.

We are told that we must have unwavering faith in order to get through to God and have our prayers answered. This is especially emphasized when it comes to prayers for the sick.

What does it mean to "have faith"? One person might say: "It means that I believe God will do whatever I ask of Him, provided I believe it strongly enough—provided I do not admit of any doubt or think of any alternative." Another person might say: "It means that I believe God will do whatever is best for me no matter what I ask, provided I trust Him implicitly and place myself in His hands." Which of these positions is more correct? Which shows a greater faith?

I once heard a speaker who is prominent among faith healers make the statement that when we pray for the sick, we must not include in the prayer the words which Jesus used in Gethsemane: ". . . not my will, but thine, be done" (LUKE 22: 42). She said that to include these words shows a lack of faith and weakens the prayer.

Certainly her view has much to commend it if we believe in auto-suggestion and mental telepathy, or if we think of God as an impersonal force which has to be manipulated in order to get Him to do that which we want. But if we think of God as a loving, personal Father—One who is conscious of every thought and need of our lives, One who is desirous of giving us the very best of everything, and One who knows more completely than we what is best for us and for those in whom we are interested—then the one who seeks the presence of God, strives to establish communion with Him, and lays every desire and petition at His feet in the fullest confidence that He will do whatever is best, is showing, by far, the greater faith.

Fourteen years ago, I was told by my doctor that I had an aneurism of the upper aorta; he said that surgery was possible, but not very reliable, and he did not recommend it; he said that with care I had several years of life before me; in fact, he said he had known people to live as long as eight or ten years with a condition as bad as mine. Naturally, I was concerned, and I took the matter to God. But for some reason it did not occur to me to ask God to heal me. I only said to Him: "Lord, you know best. For forty-six years I have been trying to serve You. Perhaps I have not done too well, and You don't need me any more. If that is true, it is okay with me. I would like to go on serving You. I really enjoy it so much, and I thought that I was doing some good. But You know best, God. You take charge."

I kept right on working, just as I had before. I did not worry about my condition—in fact, I almost forgot about it. During the fourteen years since then I have served two regular pastorates, I have established one new church and brought it to self-support, I have served eleven interim ministries, and I have held eight revivals.

I went back to see the same doctor one year ago, and he found no aneurism, just a little enlargement of the aorta, he said my health was perfectly sound. I asked him: "Doctor, is it possible that the aneurism just disappeared?" He shook his head: "No," he said, "aneurisms do not disappear. Something has happened to you—a healing Power higher than man's has cured you."

We often cite the case of the rich, young ruler, and preach about money creating a barrier between man and God. But it is not only money—there are hundreds of other things—which can separate us from God. The trouble with the rich, young ruler was that he loved something else more than he loved the Master. He was not willing to surrender everything else to second place, and place God on the "throne" in his heart. Money was his great obstacle, and Jesus told him to get rid of it. In my case, the obstacle may be something else; in yours, still another. It may be even the healing of a loved one that becomes so important to us that it pushes God into a subordinate position—we see this manifest often in the conduct of people who pray for the healing of someone dear, and then when that person is not healed, they become embittered and resentful; they may even turn against God and be guilty of blasphemy. The sin of such a person is just as great as, or perhaps even greater than, that of the young man who chose his wealth and turned his back on Jesus.

Anything that I want so badly that I am not willing to trust God's judgment as to whether I should have it or not, has become too important to me, and endangers the welfare of my very soul.

Abraham was put to the supreme test when he was told to sacrifice his son Isaac. Jehovah did not permit the sacrifice to take place, but He put Abraham to the test—no one who loved father, mother, son, or daughter more than he loved God was qualified to become the progenitor of the chosen people of God.

Jesus said: "He who loves father or mother more than me is

not worthy of me; and he who loves son or daughter more than me is not worthy of me" (MATTHEW 10:37). Jesus meant no disrespect for family ties—in fact, we find Him exalting them, and placing major emphasis on the unity of the family and the mutual respect and love that binds one to the other. He was just saying that one cannot place father, mother, son, or daughter ahead of God, and if life should ever demand a choice between them, then God must come first.

One of the most beautiful stories of complete surrender to God I have ever read is that of Catherine Marshall, as told in her book *A Man Called Peter*. Early in her married life, Catherine Marshall was stricken with tuberculosis. Both she and her husband believed implicitly in the power of prayer. They both prayed for her healing, but healing did not come. In fact, she grew steadily worse, and the doctors gave her no hope of recovery. There was so much she wanted to do for the Lord; she pleaded with Him to give her the strength to do it, but God seemed deaf to her pleadings.

At last she said: "Lord, I've done everything I've known how to do, and it hasn't been good enough. I'm desperately weary of the struggle of trying to persuade You to give me what I want. I'm beaten, whipped, through. If you want me to be an invalid for the rest of my life, all right. Here I am. Do anything You like with me and my life." Soon after she made that surrender to God she felt His healing power enter into her body, and she knew that she was going to get well.

There is such a thing as making one's health or that of a loved one paramount in our thoughts and desires, to the extent that they crowd God out. When we do that, we lose our contact with Him, and, no matter what the results of our prayers, we have lost.

When we pray for the sick, we pray in faith, we pray with all of the insistence of which we are capable, we pray as though everything depends on getting that for which we are asking. God understands all of this. He makes allowances for our human weaknesses. I think He really admires us for coming to Him and feeling free enough, in His presence, to press for something we feel is important. But He also wants us to love Him enough, to trust Him sufficiently to leave the matter in His hands, and to be able to say: "All right, Father, now I have laid my pleadings before You. I leave the matter in Your hands. I trust Your goodness and love. I know You will do that which is best for all concerned."

"True faith" is trusting God, not to do what we want done, but to do that which He knows is best; it is the awareness that as long as we are in His hands, we will be given the guidance and strength we need.

6. SHOULD WE PRAY FOR FAITH?

"PRAYER" IS NOT a free-lunch counter, nor a bargain basement, where one gets something for nothing. Prayer pays big dividends—but in order to receive dividends, an investment must be made. The returns are vastly greater than the investment, and many times of a surprisingly different and infinitely more precious nature. In prayer, as in everything else in life, effect follows cause.

In order to get through to God in prayer, one must believe "... that he exists and that he rewards those who seek him" (HEBREWS 11:6). An unbeliever may, in a moment of crisis, experience faith, and be able to pray truly. It is not for us to pronounce judgment. But it is plain and simple to understand that unless we recognize the existence of a personal God, any pretense of prayer to Him is a mockery.

Not only must we believe in the existence of God, we must believe also that He rewards those who seek Him. In other words, we must believe that God is living, that He takes account of each one of us, and hears our prayers and acts upon them. We must believe that He is a God who understands us and loves us—one to whom compassion and mercy come as naturally as breathing to us; One to whom everything is known, even the sparrow that falls.

In order to have power in prayer, we must have faith in His promises and be willing to act upon them. We must accept that with Him there is ". . . no variation or shadow due to change" (JAMES 1:17); that He is ". . . the same yesterday and today and for ever" (HEBREWS 13:8).

We must have the faith of the little girl who, playing around on the deck of her father's ship, wanted to go down in the hold where he was working. Approaching the open hatch, she called: "Daddy, I want to go down where you are."

The father, stretching out his strong arms, said to her: "All right, Darling, jump."

"But," she cried, "it is dark down there. I cannot see you. I am afraid."

"Don't be afraid," replied the father. "You cannot see me, but I can see you. Jump." And, with faith in her father's love and understanding, she leaped into his outstretched arms.

How does one come to have faith in God? Too often we hear people—especially young people—say: "I wish I had faith like that, but I don't, and I do not know how to get it." We all had a kind of faith in God when we were children, but when the naiveté of childhood left us, much of our faith in God went also, and, either through ignorance or an unwillingness to put forth the effort, both parents and church leaders failed to recognize the danger and build a more solid, creative faith.

What is faith?—Faith is not something we possess in the same sense that we "possess" a bank account, an education, or an opinion. "Faith" is not the same as "belief"—it is much more than a storing up of knowledge about something, thinking it logically through, and therefore believing.

There are millions of people in the world who have material wealth, who have education, who hold violently to opinions, and who even have certain beliefs, but they do not have an anchoring faith, and their whole lives are unstable, unpredictable, and undependable. In other words, they are failures as far as creative life is concerned. Lacking faith in material forces of the world, they never adventure; lacking faith in their fellowman, they become cynics; lacking faith in themselves, they become miserable, vacillating cowards who flee from the responsibilities of life; and lacking faith in God (thus an anchor for their spiritual "spark-of-God" beings), they wander and drift through their earthly lives, bringing neither benefit nor joy to the world or to themselves.

We do not "possess" faith—faith "possesses" us. It takes hold of and changes our whole personality—it becomes as much a part of us as the beating of our hearts; it helps to fashion and control our hopes, fears, ambitions, desires, and dreams; it gives us determination and courage; it forces us to get up when we have fallen, enabling us to look apparent defeat "squarely in the eyes" and command it to be gone.

"Faith" is one of the chief characteristics of God—He had faith when He flung out His "arms" and scattered the stars and planets in the heavens; He had faith when He said, "Let there be light"; He had faith when He created man and placed him in the world which He had just brought into being; He had faith when He sent His Son, Jesus Christ, into the world; He had faith when He let that Son die on a cross; God still has faith in the final consummation of His work and the salvation of mankind.

While "love" is greater than either "hope" or "faith," they all three are essential factors of life; and none can exist without the others. In fact, "faith" is a prerequisite of "love"—it might be said that "faith" is the minor constellation which sweeps away the clouds in order that the greater "love" may shine through. Without faith, love is impossible.

Since "faith" is such an essential part of God, then it is also a necessary part of man, in order that there may be harmony, fellowship, and rapport between God and man.

Christ was not just arbitrarily establishing a condition when He said that if one has faith, he may ask this or that and God will do it. The writer of Hebrews was not just talking idly when he said: ". . . without faith it is impossible to please him [God]" (HEBREWS 11:6). These are fundamental truths.

Doubtless the most humiliating experience in the lives of the apostles was their attempt, and failure, to heal the epileptic boy brought to them in the absence of the Master. According to Jesus, their failure was due to their "little faith" (MATTHEW 17:14-20). Jesus was not speaking of "faith" as something which the apostles did or did not possess, as an instrument which they could manipulate as a doctor manipulates a scalpel or prescribes pills—He was speaking of it as a condition of their spiritual being. "Faith" had not sufficiently possessed them so that God's power could flow through them into the body of the tortured lad—their faith was not sufficiently vital and alive.

From whence comes faith?—Near the end of his Gospel, the Apostle John made the statement that of the many things Jesus said and did, he had selected certain ones and written them ". . . that you may believe that Jesus is the Christ, the Son of God, and that believing you may have life in his name" (JOHN 20:31).

In Romans we are told that ". . . faith comes from what is heard, and what is heard comes by the preaching of Christ" (ROMANS 10:17). In this same chapter of the Roman Letter (vv. 13, 14), faith and, thus, salvation are made dependent upon hearing and accepting the word of God.

From these and other passages it can be shown that "faith"

must be built on a solid foundation of knowledge. The search for evidence and its proper, impartial, unprejudiced evaluation and acceptance are essential to faith.

For this reason, God gave us the Bible, with its story of the tragic consequences of disobedience and sin, with its story of the struggles of fallen man to regain his place of Sonship with his Creator and God, and with its accounts of God's ceaseless efforts to reveal Himself anew to man and bring man back into fellowship with Himself.

God sent His only Son into the world to live among men—to show man the depth of God's love—to live out in person those great spiritual truths which man could never understand through only the barren media of words.

All creation is filled with the evidence of God's greatness and goodness. The deeper man delves into the vastness of the secrets of God's universe, the more evidence he unearths to establish the truths in the Bible. Man is charged with the responsibility of honestly and courageously studying this evidence, and upon that evidence building a faith in God. But a vital, living, Christian faith is much more than the intellectual acceptance of established evidence, no matter how conclusive that evidence may be.

In Hebrews 11:1 we read that ". . . faith is the assurance of things hoped for, the conviction of things not seen." Faith is spiritual, as well as intellectual, and before it can bring us very close to God, it must be able to "take wings" and carry us beyond the best that our intelligence can devise and into the presence of God. Man is both intellectual and emotional—unless these two phases of his being are kept in balance, he is liable to become either a cold machine or an unstable fanatic. If man's emotions have no solid foundation of intellectual understanding to guide them, he becomes a "ship without a rudder"; but if his intelligence has closed all the "doors" to emotion, he is more like a "rudder without a ship," and thus is spiritually unable to penetrate very far into the mysteries of the truths of God.

There are those who have the facts of the Bible at their fingertips, and yet have no living faith in God; there are others who know but little of the written facts and stated truths of the Bible or of history, and who have a faith capable of "moving mountains."

Through science, man can create a grain of wheat which under the microscope cannot be distinguished from a grain God created; each has the same chemical elements in exactly the same proportions, and yet there is a difference—The grain which man made, when placed in the ground, will rot, and the one which God created will bring forth a harvest.

Scientists can explain the functioning of our bodies, they can explain the marvels of our minds, and they can tell how body and mind work; But they cannot tell *why* they work— the element of life itself, they cannot explain.

Just as God is supernatural, so faith in him has its supernatural element. A faith based solely on intellectual conclusions drawn from gatherable evidence is barren and cold, and is more liable to lead man into fruitless theological discussion than into a spiritually rewarding communion with God.

Too often man is confused by the loose way in which the words "intelligence" and "knowledge" are used. "Intelligence" is an inherent capacity of man—it inspires him to search for knowledge, it enables him to judge facts and to weigh and classify information. "Knowledge" is the fruit of intellectual activity, and for this reason "knowledge" is always relative—that which we know today may be proven false tomorrow. It all depends on the extent and the quality of the information with which the intellect has to work; also on the capacity of the particular intellect to gather, classify, weigh, evaluate, and fit together the information it has gathered; as well as the degree of freedom from prejudice, preconceived ideas, and conclusions. Until the last possible particle of information has been gathered; until a 100% perfectly developed intellect has been found, and this intellect has been purified of all prejudice, preconceived conclusions, and unwholesome and disturbing influences; until this perfect intellect has taken this complete body of information, and without error classified, organized, evaluated, and interpreted it, and without a single flaw drawn a just conclusion from it—can we say that any body of knowledge on any subject is "absolute," and even then there might be some doubts.

"Faith" is never counter to intelligence. It quite often is counter to what man takes for knowledge, and it always goes far beyond knowledge.

If man had nothing more than the material fruits of his intelligence, his whole existence would indeed be built upon "shifting sands." But intelligence (true intelligence) has a spiritual aspect—through its spiritual nature it deals with something which cannot be described in material terms. Through that spark of life which God placed in man—a part of Himself—spiritual intelligence, if properly guided toward the Source of its being, can and does build a body of spiritual knowledge—that which we call "faith."

Faith is not something we inherit from our parents or absorb through exposure to church services; it is not a haphazard something we pick up piece by piece and throw together—faith is based on the best material information which can be gathered, plus a spiritual searching which brings us in living contact with God.

It is for this reason that faith takes precedence over information; that it can be ". . . the assurance of things hoped for, the conviction of things not seen" (HEBREWS 11:1). The source of our material knowledge is our material resources; the source of faith is none other than the Author and Ruler of all the universe. Faith does not come to us full-grown—just as our "storehouse" of knowledge has to grow, so must our faith grow. The person who comes to believe a few things about God and the spiritual life, and then thinks his faith is complete, is committing a tragic blunder. Many young people, when they go off to college, "lose" their faith—they have not been taught that faith has to be cultivated and nurtured just as much as the desire for scientific knowledge.

Faith, like prayer, is a two-way interchange between man and God. Until man is willing to approach God, God can do very little for him. But until God has taken charge and given life to man's beliefs, he does not have a real faith. Man prays not only because he *has* faith, but also because he *desires* and *seeks* a greater faith.

In the Ephesian Letter we are told: "For by grace you have been saved through faith; and this is not your own doing, it is the gift of God" (EPHESIANS 2:8). Faith is the channel through which we come into possession of the salvation so generously provided by the grace, mercy, and love of our heavenly Father. It is the media through which we permit ourselves to be possessed again by God—by which we surrender ourselves to Him and permit Him to control and fill our lives. But this kind of creative, living faith is not something that man can work out by himself. It is not the result of a syllogism, no matter how logically worked out. This kind of faith is the result of cooperation between man and God.

Man must desire faith before he can be possessed of it—he must be willing to put forth an effort to know God and His will concerning man; he must hunger and thirst for a fellowship with his heavenly Father. But none of these can ever be perfected in him until God takes over and gives to him strength in place of his weakness, courage in place of his cowardice, assurance in place of his fear, and conviction to master his doubts.

Should a person pray for faith?—When Jesus said to the father of the epileptic boy: ". . . 'All things are possible to him who believes,' " the father responded: ". . . 'I believe; help my unbelief!' " (MARK 9:23, 24). That man should do everything he is able for himself is absolutely necessary, but it is never adequate.

No human is wise enough to understand all of the treasure-house of spiritual truth contained in the Bible. Without the guidance of the Holy Spirit, man is incapable of penetrating the fullness of the revelation which God has given to him. There is much to be learned from a literary study of the Bible; there is much to be gained from a study of it as "history" or as a "moral guide." But the person who approaches the Bible with nothing more than his own intellectual capability to guide and enlighten him, will rarely find that which will draw him closer to God. The Bible, if it is to reveal its spiritual message, must be studied prayerfully. Beyond its words one must seek the presence and the revealing "voice" of God.

The same is true of prayer. Perhaps man's greatest prayer should always be a prayer for greater faith and confidence in God.

In the Thessalonian Letter we are told to "pray constantly" (I THESSALONIANS 5:17), or, as the King James version states it,, more impressively, "Pray without ceasing."

"The "constant" or "ceaseless" longing of every soul should be for a close fellowship with God, for more faith and assurance, for a willingness to commit oneself more completely to the leading of God, for a more "at-oneness" or "at-homeness" with the Source of all complete and triumphant living.

It is somewhat pretentious of man to come to God with the attitude: "Lord, I come to You with the necessary faith. I have done my part; now, God, You do Your part." There is much similarity between this sort of person and the man in the parable of Jesus who stood in the temple and thanked God that he was not like other men—that he fasted and tithed and washed his hands.

Just as Jesus commended the publican who prayed simply and humbly: "God, be merciful to me, a sinner," I can imagine God being pleased with the man who comes to Him in reverence and humility and with an abiding faith, praying simply: "God, help my faltering faith," and leaving the matter of every other need in the hands of a loving Father and God.

Faith and action.—A faith which has the power to uplift man is a faith which moves him to action.

In his book *Foundation of Method,* Dr. William H. Kilpatrick many years ago propounded the question: "When can you say that a child has learned to tie his shoes?" He may have mastered the mechanical ability to go through the motions, and, when father and/or mother is standing over him, he may be able to form the knot, but he cannot be said really to know how to tie his shoes until he willingly puts on the shoes and proceeds to tie the laces.

In the same way, we might say that man does not have faith until it has sufficiently possessed him so that he wants to do something about it. The prayer of faith is not a prayer in which we sit back and expect God to do everything for us. The true prayer of faith is the prayer which stirs up our souls and drives us forth to bring to pass that which we are convinced God wants done.

Vital faith in God puts into man something of the mind of

God. When we read these words of Paul: "So faith, hope, love abide, these three; but the greatest of these is love" (I CORINTHIANS 13:13), we are prone to think of three separate entities, each complete and alone in itself. But this can never be—it is impossible to have "hope" without "faith," or "love" without both "hope" and "faith."

"Faith-hope-love" form a trinity very much like the Trinity of the godhead—separate, and yet essentially and actually One; inseparable, and yet different manifestations. "Love" is supreme in the same sense that the "Father" is supreme over the "Son" and the "Holy Spirit." "Love" is "hope" and "faith" raised to the nth power.

We are told that "God is love" (I JOHN 4:8). Therefore, God is "hope" and "faith." When we are possessed by true "hope" and "faith" and "love," we are possessed by God; and the portion of Himself placed within us when He made us "in His own image and likeness," when He made us "a little lower than God," becomes more dominant and aggressive, and we think, feel, and react more like Him. We become more concerned, restless, and willing to give of ourselves and all that we have in order that there may be accomplished in the world that for which God gave His only Son—that which brought Jesus Christ into the world and made Him willing to go to the cross.

It is very, very true that we are saved "by grace" through faith (EPHESIANS 2:8), and yet we know that "faith" without works "is dead" (JAMES 2:17). We can never perform works enough to merit salvation—this is a gift of God. On the other hand, anyone who has faith sufficient to bring him into the circle of the pardoning, saving grace of God can never sit idly by and see the task for which Christ came into the world go unfinished—he will have to be ". . . about his Father's business." (LUKE 2:49)

James told us that faith, if it fails to produce works, is not only dead, but that faith is "completed by works" (JAMES 2:22). In other words, a faith that does not stimulate us to get up and do something about cooperating with God in seeing that His will for mankind is done, is nothing more than a theoretical, wishful-thinking kind of faith. Just as the muscles of the body cannot develop and grow strong without exercise, so our faith can only be flabby and weak and unsatisfying until it is completed and made vital and strong through exercise.

James challenged all believers in Christ to demonstrate their faith by what they do (JAMES 2:18). It would be most wholesome to the Christian world today to be put to that test.

It would be a most revealing test to apply the same rule to our praying. How do our prayers change us? What do they make us do? A prayer that is not backed up by the living of the one who prays, like faith without works, is dead.

"Faith" and "prayer" are built each on the other—we cannot pray unless we possess some element of faith, but we cannot have a real, living faith without prayer. The two must not only go together, but they must also grow together.

7. PRAYER AND SELF-SURRENDER

PRAYER, LIKE LIFE itself, is a "partnership" between God and man—man is the instrument, and God is the wisdom and strength. God has given to man abilities far beyond anything he has ever realized, and God is constantly challenging man to undertake greater and greater things for Him.

God promises to do two things—He promises to give man the necessary strength and guidance (II CORINTHIANS 12:8, 9), and He promises to take responsibility for success and failure (MATTHEW 6:33, 34). He asks man to accept His challenge to break the "shackles" of conformity and fear, and venture forth with confidence and courage, as did Abraham when he broke the ties of family, homeland, and religion, and went forth with nothing more solid than the promise of God that He would make him the father of a new nation and would bring him to a city the Builder and Maker of which was God.

Perhaps the most paralyzing force in the world is the fear of failure; and close behind it is the unwillingness of man to put forth his best effort.

Sometimes we catch a vision of something really great, an overpowering, creative idea flashes through our minds, or a great challenge comes to us. For a brief period our souls are on fire, and we are restless to go, but then we begin to analyze and examine. Questions creep into our thinking: "Will I be able to see it through?" "What if I should undertake it and fail?" Our questionings make cowards of us, and our dreams lay dormant.

Practically everyone of us could have made a much larger contribution to human progress had we possessed the courage and the faith to act in that crusade to which God called us during a moment of inspiration—had we picked up the "gauntlet" and carried forward the battle when we stood at the crossroads of decision. We could have written that book, perhaps a better book than has ever been written, if we had only explored that idea, dug deep enough, and put our hearts, minds, and souls into it; but we were timid and afraid—afraid of failure.

Man has the idea that there is disgrace in failure. He fails to remember that the only disgrace is in not trying or, once the "battle" is on, not doing his best. Some of life's greatest victories have come from efforts which, for the moment, looked like failure, and some of the world's greatest benefactors died without knowing the magnitude of the blessings which they brought to mankind.

In the eyes of the world of His time, Jesus Christ was a failure. His most intimate followers once felt that a hopeless night of defeat had engulfed their dreams for a day of salvation, and they turned, discouraged and beaten, back to their nets.

There are two things which prayer should do for us—it should relieve our tensions, take away our worries, so that the powers which God has placed within us can be loosened and permitted to function at their best; it should also relieve us of any concern for the outcome of our undertakings. If we pray to God in faith, then to be overly concerned and worried about the outcome should be impossible.

We worry about the things concerning which we are uncertain. But if we are uncertain, then we are demonstrating that we do not have faith.

"But," someone might say, "what if we are praying for something that God does not want to grant?" In that case, we should rejoice that it is not granted. Again, there is no reason to worry. If I thought that God would grant something which He, in His infinite wisdom and love, knew was unwise for me, then I would have reason for deep concern; but I know He will not. Leaving results to God does not weaken our efforts, but, rather, strengthens them. No one can get that close to God without being inspired and strengthened. The fact that one recognizes that he is an instrument of God fills him with the desire to give God his very best; but until he comes to understand and trust God, he is so burdened with fears and worries that it is impossible for him to do his best.

Ministers have, perhaps, more things to try their souls and bring discouragement and a desire to retreat from it all than anyone else. Preaching, to the average minister, is not work—it is one of the most thrillingly satisying experiences of his life. Visitation, for most ministers, is time-consuming, but a fruitful and pleasant part of his daily life. The things that try his soul are the stories he hears at the counseling table, the broken homes, the neglected children, the wasted lives, the hunger, the unrest, and the injustice all about him. What really shatters his composure, takes away his courage, and sometimes makes him want to give up and run away from it all, are the petty jealousies, the gossip, the bickering, the divisions, and even the hates, which he finds among people who are supposed to be followers of Christ.

Unless he is able to place matters in the hands of God, and lie down and sleep, he is apt to wind up either a nervous wreck or out of the ministry. The fact that so few ministers do drop out and go into some other form of work, speaks in thunderous tones for the high quality and deep consecration of the Christian ministry. Unless they live very close to God and spend much time with Him in prayer, they would not be able to carry on.

Worry and fear paralyze our forces and make it impossible for us to do our best work. Consider, for example, the case of Henry G., a man of more than average ability, with a very pleasing personality. He was connected with a large organization, an organization in which there were many opportunities for advancement, but Henry did not advance. Promotions passed over him and went to someone else. Family affairs were getting in bad shape because his wife, knowing his abilities, began to nag him about his failure to gain promotions. He attended a prayer group we were conducting, and asked that we pray for him. As we talked his situation over, we learned that he was timid and uncertain of himself—he was apologetic and afraid.

We asked him: "Do you believe in the power of prayer?"

He answered: "I don't know. It does things for other people, but it does not seem to do anything for me."

The first half of the meeting comprised Bible study and exchanges of experiences. Gradually, during the twelve-month period, development and growth came to Henry G. His work at the office improved, and management began to take notice of him.

One night he came to the group and said: "There is an important position open at the office; I am to be interviewed tomorrow. Pray for me."

We asked: "Do you think you are capable of filling that job?"

He answered: "I am the best man in the organization for it."

Then we asked: "Do you think if we pray, God will help you to get it?"

"I know He will," was the reply.

He did get that job, and has since gone on to a more important position with a much larger corporation.

Worry, doubt and fear assassinate faith. Faith is necessary for success in prayer. Jesus once said: ". . . if you have faith as a grain of mustard seed, you will say to this mountain, 'Move hence to yonder place,' and it will move . . ." (MATTHEW 17:20). There are two things to be noted about this statement.

First: A mustard seed is vital, alive, creative. It holds within itself a God-given power, which, when liberated, produces a nesting place for the birds of the air and life-giving food for the hungry. Jesus did not use the mustard seed for his illustration because of its size, but because of the fact that so much active, positive, life-giving force is wrapped up within its tiny shell.

Second: Christ did not speak of moving a mountain because He expected His followers to go out and willy-nilly begin changing the topography of the earth—He was endeavoring to present one of the most difficult things to accomplish.

We know, however, that mountains have been removed and relocated, but not by man just sitting idle and saying: "Mountain, you move over to yonder place." This is not what Jesus meant. They have been moved by men with live, creative faith who have drawn deeply on the resources which God has given them and, with faith in something which the average man has called "impossible," have invented machinery and put it to work.

Hundreds of times Madame Curie failed in her experiments to discover radium, but her faith never faltered; on and on she worked, until at last "victory" was won. One with less faith would have given up.

Perhaps the greatest manifestations of the difference between man and the lower animals is man's God-given ability to dream dreams and see visions; his consciousness of a close relationship with the almighty, everlasting, all-wise, supreme Creator and Ruler of life; and his knowledge that he can draw on that Power for the strength and wisdom he needs in order to bring his dreams to fruition. In order to accomplish all this, he must have faith in himself, faith in what he is undertaking, and, above all, faith in God.

During the past fifteen years, I have been especially active in youth conferences. My special interest has been in recruitment, and I have talked with hundreds of young men and women who felt that they had received a call to full-time Christian service. They have, as a rule, been among the very finest in the group—consecrated and alive—but when it has come to making the full commitment, many have been afraid of not being able to stand up under the stress and strain. They have often said: "That is what I want to do. That is what I feel that God would have me do. But what if I am not able to see it through? What if I fail?" Because of doubt and fear, many have dillydallied along, unconscious of the strength within themselves and disregarding the power, wisdom, and love of God, to take and use their lives, until their interest has failed; sometimes they have even drifted away from Christ and His church.

The case of Norman B., an exceptionally talented young man, is an example. He has every qualification for the Christian ministry, except for sufficient faith in God to make him willing to place everything in God's hands and follow the divine call. He finished his undergraduate work, and did some preaching; but problems, difficulties, and doubts plagued him. He expected perfection in his church members, and forgot that the church is for sinners, not for saints. He tried all of the methods and techniques he had learned in school, but the results did not satisfy him—so he quit, and went into another type of work. But he did not get away from his troubles—he is a haunted soul.

There is another young man, who also is talented, has problems, and wanted to quit—but he did not. He went on, and is making a success. Many times he came to me, and we talked and prayed together. I remember one time in particular, when his church was about to fire him—a board meeting had been called to consider this action. He said: "If they fire me, I will be humiliated. It will be difficult for me to get another church. I will just quit."

I asked him: "What have you done?"

"Nothing," he replied, "except to preach the gospel as I understand it—as I feel Christ would have it preached."

I asked him: "Do you believe in the gospel you preach and the way you have conducted your work sufficiently so that you would repeat them the same way?"

"Yes," he replied, "It is the only gospel I know, and I believe in it. As far as my pastoral work is concerned, I know it is not perfect—I have learned some things and I would make some changes, but I have done my best and I do not feel that I have done too badly."

"Have you prayed about it?"

"Yes, but I am still worried sick. I feel frustrated, abused, and defeated."

"All right," I said, "You are going to spend the night with me, and we are going to pray this thing through until you are willing and able to leave the matter in the hands of God, and are able to lie down and sleep. You have done your best, you have dedicated your life to His work; now let Him look after results."

It was almost dawn before we went to bed, but when he came down for breakfast it was evident that he had slept, and there was an air of confidence about him. "You know," he said, "I am not concerned any more about what that church board does, because whatever it does, I feel confident that God will take care of me."

He went back to his church with a positive, confident air. He went about his church work more resolutely and creatively. The church board met on the appointed night, but, instead of firing him, it voted him a raise in salary and extended his call indefinitely. He still has problems, and he still has moments when he gets discouraged and fearful, but they do not last long. He has learned to place them all in the hands of God, and, with faith, challenge the "lions" in his pathway.

Fear saps away our initiative and strength; worry makes cowards of our dreams—the two together, deny our faith and place us on the periphery of God's help.

The triumphant life is the life which is willing to do its best, seek God's help, and then leave the results in His hands. If there is any worrying to be done, let God do it.

8. THROUGH PRAYER, VICTORY

EVERY GROUP, ESPECIALLY of young people, I have ever led on an adventure into the realm of prayer has sooner or later gotten around to a discussion of what prayer really does for a person.

Healing of the sick, to most people, is rather theoretical—it is something they read about or hear discussed, but in most cases it rarely touches them personally. Prayer for material things, like a new dress, an automobile, or a better job, has too great a tinge of commercialism—of selfishness.

As a group develops, it usually, sooner or later, gets down to the questions: "How can prayer help me to live a better, more satisfying, creative life?" "How can it help me to meet more victoriously the problems of everyday living?" "How can it help me to exemplify in my life more completely the spirit and teachings of the Christ I am endeavoring to serve?" "How can it make me a more useful child of God?"

Let us do a bit of exploring in this direction. We will not, by any means, attempt to explore the field completely here. We will only do a bit of adventuring, and trust that each individual will continue to adventure for himself.

Prayer and broken hearts.—Sorrow, disappointment, perplexity, and loss come to all people—they are part of all normal life, perhaps even a necessary part of life. In order to develop and mature, we need their discipline. The only way to escape them, even partially, is to withdraw into the escapist's world of utter unreality.

How we meet these disciplines depends on the character of the resources we have within us—the person who has nothing more than his own strength and determination is liable to break under the load; only those who have a Christian faith and are on speaking terms with God are capable, not only of overcoming, but of reaping rich rewards from the conflicts and testings of sorrow and disappointment.

Hospitals for the mentally and emotionally sick are crowded to their doors with people who are sorry for themselves—people who have given way to their feelings and, lacking a living faith in God and a knowledge of what He can do for them, have become frightened and confused.

The person who is willing to place his hand in the hand of God and be strengthened and directed by Him will find that the so-called trials and difficulties of life can be converted into stepping-stones that lead to a deeper, more meaningful, triumphant way of life—a creative happiness which has meaning and substance.

The late Dr. Edgar DeWitt Jones told the story of a visit he made to Old Trinity Church in Boston, a sanctuary made hallowed by the personality and great preaching of Phillips Brooks. As he knelt in the semidarkness of the sanctuary, he thought that he was alone; but suddenly he heard the sobbing of a woman—a woman crying as only a woman can when her heart is bruised and broken. His eyes now accustomed to the fading light, he saw across the aisle and a few rows ahead of him a woman, kneeling in prayer. Her face was buried in her hands, and her shoulders were shaking convulsively as she sobbed. At last the sobbing ceased, and she arose and walked down the aisle towards the exit. A shaft of light silhouetted her head and shoulders as she passed close by him—her head was held high and there was the serenity of triumph on her face; her shoulders were erect as she marched out resolutely to face the realities of life. "Her knees had found the altar stairs that slope through darkness up to God" (*Sermons I Love to Preach*).

When the late King George VI of England lay dying, the queen, heartbroken and lonely, arose early one morning, and made her way to the church for meditation and prayer. When she returned to her carriage, a photographer snapped a picture of her. It was circulated around the world, and became one of the most famous pictures of the queen. The remarkable thing about it was the expression of serenity, courage, and victory on her face. Not only her King, but, her husband, the father of her children, was dying; but she had just held a rendezvous with God, and her soul was at peace.

One of the most precious invitations in all of the Bible is that of Jesus when he said: "Come to me, all who labor and are heavy laden, and I will give you rest. Take my yoke upon you, and learn from me; for I am gentle and lowly in heart, and you will find rest for your souls" (MATTHEW 11:28, 29). In simple, understandable words he told us that if we are tired and discouraged, if we are loaded down by sorrow and disappointment, if things have gone wrong, and its seems like the world is caving in on us, "come to Me—enter into fellowship with Me, try to become like Me, let My spirit enter into you, learn how I meet problems and still remain victorious, and you will find victory, freedom from worry, and ever-increasing strength."

One of the most frequently repeated words in the Old Testament is "refuge." Over and over again it is repeated, as in Psalm 46:1-3: "God is our refuge and strength, a very present help in trouble. Therefore we will not fear though the earth should change, though the mountains shake in the heart of the sea; though its waters roar and foam, though the mountains tremble with its tumult."

Prayer and guidance.—One of the least understood and appreciated fruits of fellowship with the Infinite is in the realm of guidance. We are told in Isaiah 58:11: "And the Lord will guide you continually. . . ." One of the missions of the Spirit of Truth, or Holy Spirit, if you will, is to guide us ". . . into all the truth . . ." (JOHN 16:13).

A missionary friend of mine arrived in New York late one Saturday night. He had been told by his mission board that he was to speak the next morning in a church in Brooklyn, but neither the name of the church nor the name and address of the minister were given. He searched the telephone directories to no avail (he later found that, unfamiliar with the great city, he had looked in the wrong directories). Being Saturday night, church offices were closed, and the two people he knew in the city did not answer their phones.

When he could think of nothing else to do, he prayed. Then he went to bed, and had a good night's sleep. The next morning he was up early; and, without eating breakfast, boarded an elevated train for Brooklyn. He just kept riding until something told him it was time to get off. While he was in a little restaurant eating breakfast, he heard a church bell ringing. One block away he found a Lutheran church; in answer to his inquiry the Lutheran minister pointed down the street to another church, and said: "I think that is the church you are hunting." It was. Brooklyn is a big place. What was it that told him to get off the train at that particular stop? It certainly was not an accident.

I had a similar experience some years later. Expected mail failed to reach me in New York City. I was scheduled to be in Albany on Sunday and in Rochester on Wednesday night—that left Monday and Tuesday free. For some reason, I had an urge to go to Watertown. I had no reason for this; the fact is, I knew very little about that city. I arrived in Watertown late on Monday afternoon, checked in at a hotel, bought a paper, and went to my room. Adjusting myself in a big, comfortable chair, I opened my paper. The very first item my eyes fell on was a notice that I was to speak in Carthage, a few miles away, on Tuesday night.

Why did I go to Watertown? That is the only place where the notice would have reached me. Even if I had gone to Carthage, instead of Watertown, I would not have seen the notice, because Carthage did not have a daily paper. Was it an accident? It would be very difficult to convince me that it was.

On Wednesday in Rochester, the mail which had missed me in New York City caught up with me, and there was a letter saying that I was scheduled to speak in Carthage on Tuesday night.

Prayer and clear thinking.—The human mind is one of the greatest mysteries in all of life—how it functions and what it is capable of doing—memorizing (the mind's capacity for recalling data); evaluating, organizing facts, and drawing conclusions; making decisions. Only a wise, all-powerful, eternal Creator could have brought into being such a complicated, delicately balanced, powerful instrument.

Since the human mind is the creation of God, it naturally functions best when it is in harmony with God, and when it is subject to His influence and direction. Prayer has been found, by millions of people, to be the best stimulus to clear, creative thinking. It has proven the most effective remedy for clearing away the "cobwebs" from our mental processes. The God who created the mind and ordained its modus operandi is certainly the One most capable of keeping it functioning at its best.

In our group discussions, numerous examples of how prayer helped clear the mind were offered. One was related by a young professor, who told of the mental fatigue he felt as he approached the oral examination for his doctorate. He was convinced that he knew his subjects. He had worked hard, and was confident of his ability. But as the day for the examination approached, he felt mentally weary, his thinking was fuzzy, and his reactions were slow.

A few hours before he was to meet the committee, he went into the university chapel, and knelt at the altar in prayer. Gradually, as he communed with God, his mind began to clear, his thinking became sharp, and facts and ideas came into proper focus.

He passed the examination without difficulty, and, instead of being nervous, he really enjoyed the interchange of ideas with his professors.

Two college sudents told of being lost in the North Carolina mountains. Entranced by the beauty and grandeur of the scenery, they penetrated deep into an uncharted area, and completely lost the trail. Neither was an experienced woodsman; as the afternoon wore on, they became deeply concerned, and then downright frightened. All sense of direction deserted them, and nothing looked familiar.

At last one of them said: "Let us pray about it." And they did. Sitting down at the foot of a tree, they spent perhaps fifteen minutes in prayer. When they opened their eyes and stood up, they found that they were within ten feet of the trail. Their sense of direction was regained, and they proceeded, with no more difficulty, to their camp.

In their confusion, they had crossed the trail several times without recognizing it. That season of prayer had taken away their panic, cleared their thinking, and brought things back into proper perspective.

Prayer and manual skills.—A prominent surgeon once told me that he always prays before performing an operation. He says that prayer not only clears his mind, but helps his hand to be steadier, and enables him to proceed with greater assurance and courage.

He told of one case in particular. He had been up most of the night before; he was tired, and his nerves were jumpy. He had to perform a difficult emergency operation. He first thought of taking something to calm his nerves, but he knew that this would tend to make him less alert, and he ruled it out. Five minutes before the operation he sat at his desk, bowed his head in his hands, and asked God to take over and give him the composure and strength he needed.

"It seemed," he said, "that a hand was placed on my shoulder, and strength began to flow into and through my body. Fatigue vanished, and confidence and composure came in. In the operating room," he continued, "my reflexes were sharp, and my hands steady. I knew there was a Power present that was greater than, and outside of, my own."

The operation was a success; but fifteen minutes after it was over, the surgeon collapsed, and had to be put to bed. For the emergency there had been provided a Source of power which carried him through.

A baseball pitcher told the story of the day his curves were not breaking properly. The game was extremely important, but he seemed to have nothing "on the ball." He called upon every physical resource within him, but balls were being hit all over the field. Between innings he withdrew to one side and prayed. He knew that he had the skill, but today it was not working.

As he prayed, he felt composure coming back to him. His muscles became more relaxed. He walked back to the mound with an inner assurance, and shut out the opposition for the rest of the game.

A television set can pick out of the air pictures and sounds which originate miles, and now by way of Telstar thousands of miles, away. However, the set has to be tuned properly. Man, when properly tuned to God, has within his reach powers of which he has never dreamed.

Prayer and the control of fear.—Some years ago, a young minister found it necessary to travel from one western town to another quite a distance away. There was no public transportation which could get him there in time for his engagement. The son of a brother minister worked at the airport, and offered to take him in a borrowed plane.

When the young man appeared with the plane, the minister became a bit concerned, because it looked rather battered. But, not wanting to appear ungrateful, he said nothing.

After they were in the air and on their way, the young pilot told him that he did not have a license, and also that he had taken up flying because he had been shell-shocked in the war, and the psychiatrist had recommended it as an outlet for his tangled nerves.

The combination of all these things threw a real scare into the minister. But it was too late to do anything about it. So he prayed. "After being dumb enough to get myself into such a mess, I was ashamed to ask God to bring me down safely," he said, "so I just asked Him to take away all fear and concern. In a little while," he went on, "I found myself leaning back and really enjoying the trip. I got happier thrills out of that trip than from any other flight. The feeling came over me," he continued, "that if we got down safely, there was nothing to worry about. And if this was to be my last ride, I wanted to die happy. All anxiety and fear were gone."

When he told the story in later years, the young minister always added: "After that experience, I could in a small way, better understand how the early martyrs could face hungry lions with songs on their lips." Prayer can really cast out fear.

We could go on and on with incidents of the transforming, sustaining, inspiring powers of prayer. We have sown the seed; the reader can, from his own experience, add to this list. The additions will grow both in number and meaning as the reader grows in his fellowship with God.

As an individual grows spiritually, he finds that prayer becomes a way of life—not just something to turn to when there is a special need or desire. As he becomes more at ease in the presence of the Almighty, he will find it easier to reach out and touch the "hem" of His "garments," and feel the continuous flow of inspiration, strength, and guidance into his being.

There will never come a time when a child of God does not have to go to Him with special problems and requests; but the ultimate goal towards which we all strive is to live so close to God that, as needs arise, there can be an immediate inflow of power and direction. This is doubtless what the writer of the Thessalonian Letter had in mind when he said to "pray constantly."

Prayer is not a "court of last resort"—it is, rather, man's "first," the "refuge" to which he automatically turns. It is easy to talk to the person who is in constant communion with his heavenly Father about the things most intimately related to life—its triumphs as well as its problems. The person who has a continuous, open line to the Fountainhead of power has no difficulty finding Him when a crisis arises, and he is more apt to find the consolation, guidance, and strength he needs.

9. SUMMARY

Why should I pray?—Praying is an essential characteristic of man. It is as natural as breathing and, at times, as unconscious. Every man does and must, by his nature as a human being, pray—the savage in the jungle; the trained scientist in his laboratory; one who never goes to a church, one who claims that he is an agnostic, or an active church member; one who lives in a hovel where the struggle for physical survival is so great that his major attention is directed towards obtaining food for his empty stomach, or one who lives in a mansion with the fruits of abundance heaped about him. Prayers are always directed to some superior Power, a Power which man hopes can and will do for him that which he cannot do himself.

At some time and at some place, every man feels the desire and the irresistible urge to pray—when, seemingly, the world is caving in on him, or when he stands trembling on the brink of his greatest success; when sorrow and tragedy stare him in the face, or in that hour of enchantment when a nurse places his newborn child in his arms and says, "Both mother and child are doing fine"; when he walks through the dirty slums of a city, with its haggard-faced women, its discouraged men, and its uncared-for children, or when he stands atop a lofty mountain and views with choking emotion the peace and serenity of the valley below; when he bends low, with an aching back, tilling the soil, or when he stands at the end of the day, watching the glory of a sunset.

What is prayer?—There are different levels of prayer. The most common, and also the least rewarding, is the prayer for "things"—for material blessings. Jesus did not tell us not to pray for things; but He did say that it is useless, because God already knows what we need before we pray—He implied that God, knowing what we need, is willing and anxious to give them, provided we are prepared to receive them.

The highest type of prayer is that of "communion"—of spiritual fellowship with God. It is letting Him talk to us; it is opening the "doors" of our hearts and letting Him come in; letting Him take control of our lives, and guide, direct, and use us. Our most sincere, effective prayers are too spiritual to be placed in human words—God can read the depth of the longings of our souls.

Lord, teach us to pray.—The prayer which Jesus gave to his followers, the Lord's Prayer, is not a prayer just to be repeated, but is primarily an outline for man to follow in his personal praying. It sets up certain principles to be followed—the brotherhood of man; the evangelization of the world; the lack of anxiety over material things; the willingness to forgive, just as we are forgiven; the consciousness that in order to live uprightly, we need help. With these principles in mind, we are to fashion our prayers. Until we get beyond mere repetition of the words and become conscious of the breadth, depth, and the spiritual all-inclusiveness of this prayer, we have not learned the lesson which Jesus was seeking to give.

Whatsoever you ask in His name.—There is no magic in the phrase "in the name of Christ." Attaching it to the end of a petition is meaningless. While Christ said: "Whatever you ask in my name, I will do it (JOHN 14:13) . . . , He also said: "If you abide in me and my words abide in you, ask whatever you will, and it shall be done for you (JOHN 15:7)." God does not promise to grant frivolous petitions, but, if we are sufficiently acquainted with God and sufficiently in accord with His spirit, we will know how to ask for the things which God can provide for us.

Prayer for the sick.—There is nothing mysterious about spiritual healing—it is a natural thing. When we realize the nature of man and his true relationship to God, the mystery is that this power of healing is so seldom used. The mind and emotions of man must be organized in order to function properly; in order for them to be organized, they must have a center; being spiritual creatures, we must have a spiritual center; in order to have a spiritual center for our lives, we must know God; in order to know God, we must spend time with Him, we must have faith in Him, and we must cultivate an at-oneness with Him. Getting out of touch with God makes people both spiritually and physically ill.

If getting out of touch with God can make us ill, then getting in touch with Him can make us well. If fear, envy, jealousy, suspicion, and hate can make us physically ill—and they do—then replacing these with faith, hope, and love can make us well.

The healing power of God goes much further. If, in the normal course of things, peace, confidence, faith, and love in fellowship with God can bring health and well-being, then what can be the limitations when God increases His presence, and more completely anoints us with His strength and care?

Why God does not heal every illness we do not know. Is it because He has certain laws beyond which He will not go? Is it because there is something in the life of the sick one which impedes His entrance? Is it that there are counter forces involved which block the full working of His presence? Is it that, in His infinite wisdom, He knows that something else is better? We do not know. There are a world of things in life which we do not understand, some of them the very simple facts of everyday life.

There is one thing, however, that we know—that God can and does heal millions of people, some of them with diseases pronounced incurable by the best, most reliable doctors.

Should we pray for faith?—Man must learn how to pray, even though he is a praying being—it is part of his nature. He is born with a necessity to pray, but he is not born with an understanding of either the full nature or the possibilities of prayer. Through experience and effort man has to learn to pray. The parent who takes it for granted that his child will automatically grow up to understand and appreciate the value and the possibilities of prayer is greatly mistaken. The church that neglects the development of the prayer life of its people is liable to become anemic and spiritually ineffective. Through experience and experimentation, we learn to find God, and to enter into communion and fellowship with Him. We also learn the difference between prayers of the lips and prayers of the heart.

Prayer and self-surrender.—We must be honest with God. In prayer, as in everything else, absolute sincerity is essential —we can not fool Him. No matter what is on our lips, God knows what is in our hearts. We must be honest and sincere, and we must also be willing to do our part in the fulfillment of our prayers. We can not seek something, and then sit down and expect God to do it all. God only takes over when we have reached the limit of our enlightenment and strength. After we have done our part, or until we are well into the process of doing it, then God steps in.

With prayer as our resource, we must live a day at a time. It is useless—even destructive—to have regrets about yesterday or forebodings about tomorrow. We must banish worry and fear from our souls, do our best, and leave the rest to God. He has promised to do two things—furnish us with guidance and strength, and be responsible for the results. After prayer, he who has a living faith should be willing to leave the worrying to God, if he thinks it necessary.

Through Prayer, Victory. If you put water, in instead of gasoline, in the tank of your automobile it will not run. If you cut the wires which connect the lighting system of your home with the main power lines, you will have no lights. Man's body, mind, spirit are capable of properly functioning when they are in harmony with their Creator. Most of our illnesses, frustrations, failures are due to a weakening, or even destruction of that harmony. Restore that harmony, and strength and direction come back. No one ever had more trials and hardships than the Apostle Paul, and yet with confidence he could say: "I can do all things in him who strengthens me." (PHILIPPIANS 4:13). Man will never know the extent of his possibilities until he comes to let God be the senior partner and have control of his life.

There are two passages of Scripture which you should keep in mind. One is Matthew 6:7,8, where Jesus said: " 'And in praying do not heap up empty phrases as the Gentiles do; for they think that they will be heard for their many words. Do not be like them, for your Father knows what you need before you ask him.'"

The other passage is Matthew 6:33: "But seek first his kingdom and his righteousness, and all these things shall be yours as well."

Foster parents were taking their little newly adopted son home with them. On the way from the orphanage the little fellow was silent and sad. When they reached their home, and were settled, the father said to his newly acquired son: "Johnny, what do you most want? Tell me, and I will do my best to give it to you."

The little fellow, with tears in his eyes, looked up at his father and said: "Hold me on your lap, Daddy."

When we have reached that point in our praying where we can trust God to understand our material needs, and know that through His overwhelming love. He will provide for them, and when we are inspired, moved by His goodness and love, filled with gratitude and thanksgiving, and can say "Fold me in the arms of your tender goodness and mercy, O God, and help me to so live that I shall be able to dwell in Thy presence forever," when we can make this our prayer, then have we really learned to pray.